Master Your Body, M
Social Life

COMPLETE TEEN GUIDE TO MODERN MANHOOD

REAL TALK LIBRARY

CONTENTS

Trigger Warning v
Introduction vii

PART ONE
A TIME OF CHANGE

1. Puberty 101 3
2. What Does It Mean to Be a Man? 11
3. Friends and Family Remix 21

PART TWO
DATING, SEX, AND RESPECT

4. Crushes and Dating 35
5. Sex 101 46
6. The Real Sex Talk 54
7. Consent 66
8. The Role of Substances in Consent 70
9. Sexual Violence 74

PART THREE
THE ONLINE WORLD AND ME

10. The Internet and You 89
11. What Porn Promises 95
12. Digital Manners 98

PART FOUR
THE DANGER ZONE

13. The Sneaky Grip of Addiction 111
14. Good Decisions vs Bad Decisions 127

PART FIVE
BECOMING MY BEST SELF

15. Discovering Me 139
16. Good Decisions vs Bad Decisions 150

17. Teen Angst 157
18. Finding a Job and Managing Money 168
Answer Keys 178
19. Keep Growing, Keep Showing Up 181

Bibliography 183
About the Author 195

TRIGGER WARNING

This book contains discussions of sexual assault, substance use, and sexually explicit material for educational purposes.

INTRODUCTION

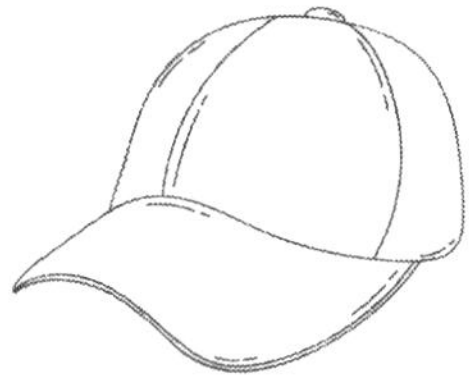

So your voice is doing weird things, you're outgrowing clothes faster than your parents can buy them, and suddenly everyone's got a view on what it means to be a man. Fun times, right?

In ancient civilisations, the journey from boy to man was more clearly mapped out. Imagine being a young warrior in Sparta your initiation into manhood would unfold through rigorous trials of strength, endurance, and honour.

In the Roman era, when a boy was ready to become a man, his father would put on a grand ceremony. The boy would remove the purple-striped toga he'd worn since childhood, shave off his first beard as an offering to the gods, and put on the plain white toga of a man.

These traditions and ceremonies gave structure to growing up, and everyone - your family, your community, your elders - knew exactly how to guide you through it.

Today most of those well-worn scripts have died out, leaving you to figure it out for yourself without a compass or a map.

Instead, there's internet throwing up a million mixed messages about what it means to be a young man. Some advice is solid gold. Some is complete garbage. And honestly? It's exhausting trying to figure out which is which.

No wonder it feels like one of the most confusing times to grow up. That's where this book comes in. Think of it as your survival guide for navigating the chaos and working out what kind of young man you want to be - the kind that gains respect and avoids embarrassment - someone other people look up to, not because you pretend to have it all together, but because you're working it out as you go along.

WHAT WE'LL COVER:

- puberty and all the chaos that comes with it
- friendship, peer pressure, and how to hold your ground without losing your crew
- dating, relationships, and what consent actually means in real life
- sex—including the big "M" word (masturbation—yup we're going there!)
- masculinity, and how to separate what's real from the toxic online noise
- the truth about porn
- digital manners—aka, how to be a gent online
- gaming, social media, and how not to let your screen own you
- dealing with anger, anxiety, and those times when you just want to shut the world out
- recognizing addiction before it becomes a real problem
- risk-taking that doesn't torch your future

- confidence, self-respect, and building your own version of success (not someone else's)
- How to earn, save, and handle your money like you've actually got plans

Becoming a young man can feel like juggling flaming swords on a moving bike. It's wild, unpredictable, and totally figure-out-able. With the right tools, you can keep your balance, own your choices, and actually enjoy the ride.

You ready? Let's do this.

PART ONE
A TIME OF CHANGE

ONE
PUBERTY 101

Puberty. You've probably heard the word in health class, during some awkward conversation with an adult, or maybe from your friends messing around like it's a joke. But nobody really tells you what it *feels* like when your own body decides to switch gears without asking first.

Puberty might feel like chaos, but it's a universal process that every guy experiences. By the end of this chapter, you'll know what's happening, why it's happening, and how to handle it like a pro.

YOUR BODY'S BIG MAKEOVER

So, what exactly is puberty? In simple terms, it's your body's way of leveling up from childhood to adulthood. Think of it like hitting a new stage in your favorite game: new challenges, cool upgrades, and maybe a few unexpected surprises. During puberty, your body gets ready for reproduction—yes, that means eventually having kids someday (no pressure, though). Here's how it works: a tiny boss in your brain called the hypothalamus sends a signal to the pituitary gland (a.k.a. the control center), and that's when the magic starts.

For boys, this process usually kicks off between the ages of 9 and 16. If you're starting earlier or later than your friends, don't sweat it —everyone's timeline is different, and there's no "right" age to begin. The main player in all this? Testosterone, the hormone that's basically in charge of flipping the puberty switch. Once your pituitary gland gives the green light, testosterone gets to work, triggering a chain reaction of physical and emotional changes.

But why does all this happen? The short answer: biology. Your body's getting itself ready for the big leagues of adulthood. Sure, it might not seem super useful right now, but every change is part of becoming the best version of yourself.

PHYSICAL CHANGES: THE FULL RUNDOWN

Alright, here's where things get interesting (and maybe a little weird —but in a good way). All those hormones we talked about earlier? They're not just hanging out—they're running the show and making big things happen. Testosterone is like the hype man for your body, calling the shots and making sure everything is leveling up.

- **The overnight stretch:** Ever feel like someone secretly stretched you out overnight? That's a growth spurt for you. Boys can grow several inches in a year, which might leave you feeling like your body is trying to catch up with itself. One minute you're borrowing your older brother's shoes, and the next, you're looking for size 12s because nothing fits anymore. It's not always graceful—you might feel gangly or uncoordinated for a bit—but it's a sure sign your body is leveling up.

- **Muscles on the rise:** Thanks to testosterone, your shoulders start to broaden, and you might notice your arms and legs getting stronger. It's like your body's subtle way of saying, "Get ready for adulthood, buddy." Bonus: your chest might even start to look more defined, which is pretty cool. Whether or not you're hitting the gym, these changes are a natural part of growing up.
- **Voice cracks and epic lows:** Ah, the infamous voice drama. One day, you're chatting with your friends, and the next, your voice cracks like it's trying to embarrass you in public. What's going on? Your vocal cords are growing, which makes your voice deeper. It's all part of the process, and soon you'll have a voice so deep you could narrate movie trailers.
- **Hair, hair everywhere:** Puberty brings hair—and lots of it. You'll notice it popping up in your armpits, on your face, and, well, other places. This isn't the light fuzz you had before; it's darker, thicker, and a little harder to ignore. Some guys can't wait to start shaving, while others take a more laid-back approach. Either way, it's another sign your body is transforming.
- **The battle with acne:** Let's talk pimples. Hormones love to mess with your skin, which is why acne is so common during puberty. Your oil glands go into overdrive, clogging pores and causing breakouts. It's frustrating, sure, but it's also temporary. A good skincare routine and a little patience can go a long way.
- **Testicle changes and erections:** Your testicles play a starring role in puberty. They start to grow, getting larger and beginning to produce sperm. This is a big deal because it's a sign your body is now capable of reproduction. Along with this, you'll likely experience

erections more often. Sometimes they'll happen without warning—yes, even in the middle of math class. It's awkward but totally normal and just another sign your body is adjusting to all these new hormonal signals.

- **Wet dreams and new feelings:** And then there's the stuff no one really talks about: wet dreams and a growing interest in sex. These experiences can feel confusing, embarrassing, or even a little scary, but they're completely normal. Wet dreams are just your body's way of adjusting to its new capabilities, and having new feelings is part of figuring out who you are.

Remember, while your body is going through these changes, your emotions are tagging along for the ride. The connection between body and mind is strong, and we'll get into the emotional side of puberty next.

WHEN YOUR EMOTIONS GO NEXT LEVEL

One minute, you're cracking up at a meme with your friends; the next, you're ready to rage-quit the group chat because someone forgot to laugh at your joke. What's going on? Welcome to the emotional rollercoaster of puberty, where your feelings are like a playlist on shuffle—one second, it's hype, the next, full-on heartbreak ballads. And no, you don't get to pick the tracks.

- **Mood swings hit different:** Puberty cranks your emotions up to ultra-HD. Little stuff suddenly feels *huge*. A bad grade? Feels like the universe is plotting against you. Your crush doesn't text back? Clearly, life as you know it is over. Everything is *so intense*, like someone turned your feelings into a reality show, complete with drama, suspense, and plot twists.

- **Finding your vibe:** You're not just dealing with mood swings—you're testing out who you are. One day, you're channeling your inner rebel, and the next, you're deep in your feels, journaling like it's your life's work. It's all about figuring out what clicks. Maybe you'll realize you're into drawing, gaming, or writing lyrics that would make Drake jealous. It's trial and error, but it's also kind of exciting.
- **The independence upgrade:** Suddenly, rules that once felt normal now seem... optional. Pushing boundaries and making your own choices are all part of the process. Sure, sometimes you'll mess up (we've all been there), but every stumble gets you closer to understanding what works for you.
- **Trying new things:** Maybe you want to try out for a sport you've never played, or maybe dye your hair neon purple just to see what it looks like. These urges to take risks are fueled by curiosity and the drive to prove you're ready to take on the world. Not every idea will be a win (RIP, questionable haircut decisions), but that's the fun of it: trying, learning, and discovering what makes you who you are.

If all this feels chaotic, it's because it is! Your brain's basically under construction, rewiring and upgrading itself to get ready for adulthood. Sure, it's messy, but every emotional surge is helping you grow into someone amazing.

HOW CULTURES CELEBRATE GROWING UP

Puberty isn't just about biology, though. Across the globe, people have been celebrating this milestone for generations in ways that are as unique as they are fascinating. These celebrations aren't just about changes—they're about marking the journey from childhood to adulthood with meaning, pride, and sometimes a little adventure. Let's explore:

Brazil

Now, let's travel to the deep Amazon rainforest with the Sateré-Mawé tribe, and you'll find a rite of passage that puts nerves (and hands) to the test. Young boys put on gloves filled with bullet ants—tiny insects with a sting so intense, it's been compared to an electric shock. It's no small feat to endure these bites; the challenge takes grit, focus, and the ability not to freak out when the pain hits. But in the eyes of the Sateré-Mawé, it's a powerful signal that a boy is ready to step up and face life head-on.

Of course, the toughest trials are followed by a well-deserved celebration. Once the ordeal is over (and the ants are safely out of sight), the community comes together with music, dancing, and generous helpings of food. There's a real sense of camaraderie, as everyone honors the strength and perseverance shown by the new initiates. Though those ant bites may leave a mark, the lasting memory is one of courage, unity, and an unshakable story to share for years to come.

Vanuatu

On Pentecost Island in Vanuatu, boys don't just talk about bravery—they prove it through a jaw-dropping ritual called land diving, or naghol. When a boy is ready to transition into manhood, he climbs a handmade wooden tower—sometimes over 100 feet tall—with only vines tied to his ankles. Then, with the whole village watching, he leaps headfirst toward the ground. The vines are measured so that his head just brushes the earth without hitting it, a symbolic connection to the land and to life itself.

To outsiders, this might sound terrifying or even dangerous. And yeah—it's intense. But for the people of Vanuatu, it's a powerful tradition rooted in courage, spiritual meaning, and ancestral pride. Completing the dive marks a boy's readiness to become a man, and the entire community comes together to celebrate his strength and bravery. Fun fact? This ritual actually inspired the invention of modern bungee jumping, though nothing beats the meaning behind the original.

Jewish Communities

In Jewish tradition, a boy's path toward adulthood is marked by a Bar Mitzvah at age 13—an event steeped in faith, family ties, and the promise of personal accountability. The centerpiece often involves reading from the Torah in front of friends and relatives, symbolizing a new level of responsibility within the community. It's a moment when a young person officially steps up, ready (at least in theory) to make choices guided by Jewish law and wisdom.

But don't let the formalities fool you—once the ceremony wraps up, the celebration kicks into high gear. Expect music, plenty of dancing, heartfelt speeches, and enough treats to keep everyone munching for hours.

From bullet ants to Torah scrolls, these traditions might not be your typical weekend plans, but they all prove that puberty is a big deal. Cultures around the world have found creative (and sometimes slightly painful) ways to say, "Hey, growing up deserves a celebration!"

Your journey might not involve ants with anger issues or ancient texts, but it's no less epic. Puberty is like your personal origin story—awkward moments, weird powers (hello, voice cracks), and all.

So, lean a bit into the chaos. Feel all the things. Growing up is supposed to be a little wild. Next, we'll see how all these changes connect to the social side of life, how you see yourself, and what it even means to be a guy. Because if emotions are confusing, figuring out masculinity can feel like its own kind of puzzle.

TWO
WHAT DOES IT MEAN TO BE A MAN?

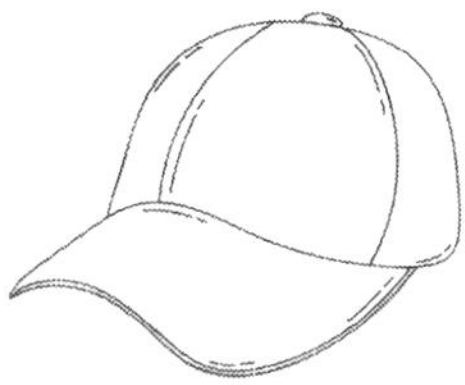

Your body is gearing up to make you a man! But what does that even mean? Is it about rocking a six-pack and having a deep voice? Holding doors open like a rom-com gentleman? Or is it about always looking fearless, like an action hero who somehow never breaks a sweat?

The thing is, being a man (and also being a woman) has always been complicated. These days, it's an ever-changing mix of tradition, modern expectations, and—most importantly—what feels right for *you*.

Look around, and you'll see all kinds of examples—your dad, your friends, your favorite athletes or actors. Some of it might feel inspiring, while some might make you cringe. That's totally normal. This chapter is all about exploring masculinity, from its strengths to its struggles, and helping you figure out what kind of man you want to be.

DECODING MASCULINITY

Masculinity is about the qualities, behaviors, and roles society associates with being male. But here's the kicker: it's not set in stone. The idea of what it means to "be a man" has shifted over time and continues to evolve.

Back in the day, masculinity was tied to big-ticket traits: strength, dominance, independence, and assertiveness. Think action heroes who never ask for help and somehow win every fight without breaking a sweat. While those traits were admired, they also came with unspoken rules—rules that boxed men into rigid roles and left little room for emotional growth or vulnerability.

But what if we looked at these traits differently? Let's take the highlights of traditional masculinity and flip the script:

- **Dominance as leadership:** True leadership isn't about bossing people around; it's about empathy, collaboration, and lifting others up.
- **Strength beyond the gym:** Physical strength is cool, but emotional strength—like resilience and standing up for others—is the real flex.
- **Independence with a side of connection:** Being self-reliant is great, but knowing when to lean on someone. That's emotional maturity.
- **Assertiveness with respect:** Speaking your mind is powerful, but kindness and respect make your voice worth listening to.

When these traits are balanced, they become tools for growth, connection, and self-respect. But when taken to extremes, they create something called toxic masculinity—the kind of mindset that says "real men" don't cry, never ask for help, and always have to dominate. This version of masculinity is more about control and fear than confidence and respect.

So, what's the alternative? Masculinity that's about balance. It's about choosing traits and behaviors that feel authentic to you while ditching outdated rules that don't fit. This isn't about reinventing the wheel; it's about rethinking what it means to be a man—on your terms.

THE MANOSPHERE TRAP

And while this all sounds great, there's a loud corner of the internet that's pushing a very different version of masculinity. One that promises to teach you how to be a "real man." On the surface, it might seem helpful—advice on confidence, self-improvement, and success sounds great, right? But underneath that shiny exterior, you'll find something darker—communities that fuel anger, resentment, and rigid ideas of what masculinity means.

What Is the Manosphere?

Here's their pitch: masculinity is in crisis, and they've got the secret sauce to fix it. Sounds intriguing, right? Except their "fix" isn't about helping you grow—it's about pointing fingers. Women? Feminism? The modern world? All apparently to blame for whatever's stressing you out. Kindness and vulnerability? They call those "weak." Instead, they're pushing dominance, aggression, and pretending your emotions don't exist. Spoiler: that's not strength. That's denial, dressed up to look cool.

And then there's their obsession with "trad wives." Heard of them? Think 1950s housewives with a TikTok filter. It's a trend popping up all over socials—women baking bread, wearing vintage dresses, and claiming life is better when they focus entirely on their husbands and homes. Sounds cozy, right? Except this fantasy skips the part where women back then had fewer choices and a lot less freedom. Sure, everyone deserves to live how they want, but let's not act like going full retro is the answer to modern problems.

Where are these ideas spreading? All the usual places: TikTok, YouTube, Reddit. The flashy videos and bold advice can seem weirdly appealing, especially if you're feeling stuck or unsure. Struggling with relationships? They'll tell you it's because women have "too many expectations." Feeling lost? They'll promise to help you "reclaim" your manhood with rigid rules and outdated ideas. It's like junk food for your insecurities: quick, tempting, but far from nourishing.

Why It Matters

The real danger isn't just what the manosphere says, it's how it makes you feel. By promoting toxic masculinity, it encourages fear over connection, control over collaboration, and anger over understanding. Here's what this might look like in real life:

- **You feel pressured to "prove" your manhood:** By rejecting anything considered "feminine," like showing emotions or asking for help.
- **You begin to see relationships as battles to win:** Rather than partnerships to build.
- **You feel isolated or angry:** Blaming others for challenges instead of finding ways to grow and connect.

This is an ideology that can creep into how you treat yourself and others. In extreme cases, it's even been linked to real-world consequences, from fractured friendships to acts of violence rooted in resentment and fear.

Being a Guy My Way

The good news? You're not stuck listening to outdated, toxic advice about being a man. Even better? Breaking away from the harmful ideas of the manosphere doesn't require you to participate in online battles! You can make smarter choices about what you consume, share, and believe. Here's how:

1. Curate Your Feed

Think of social media as your digital wardrobe. If your feed is full of negativity, it's like wearing socks with holes—they're not doing you any favors. Swap out the bad vibes for creators who promote empathy, growth, and respect.

- **Follow creators who inspire, not divide:** Look for people sharing real-life advice, encouraging self-improvement, or spreading positivity.
- **Unfollow the noise:** Accounts pushing anger, resentment, or rigid stereotypes. Hit that unfollow button. Your peace of mind is worth it.
- **Think before you share:** If something feels off—too aggressive, too judgmental—it probably is. Sharing responsibly is part of breaking the cycle.

2. Question, Don't Clash

When you hear something that doesn't sit right, take a moment to ask questions instead of jumping into a heated debate.

- **Ask thoughtfully:** Try, "What makes you think

that?" or "Have you looked at it this way?" Curiosity invites conversation without starting a war.

- **Set the tone:** If a friend says something toxic, you can respond with, "Here's why I see it differently." Calm but clear is the way to go.
- **Know your limit:** If someone's not willing to engage respectfully, it's okay to bow out. You're not responsible for changing everyone's mind.

3. Don't Fear Feminism

Here's where the manosphere gets it all wrong: feminism isn't the enemy of masculinity—it's an ally. The real goal of feminism is equality, and that benefits everyone, including you.

- **Understand what feminism really is:** It's about breaking down stereotypes that hold both men and women back.
- **Spot everyday sexism:** From dismissive jokes to unfair expectations, recognizing inequality is the first step to rejecting it.
- **Be the ally you'd respect:** Supporting fairness doesn't make you less of a man; it makes you someone others admire and trust.

4. Make Masculinity Your Own

The manosphere tries to convince you there's one way to be a man: tough, emotionless, and always in control. Forget that. Masculinity is what *you* make it.

- **Pick what works for you:** Traits like confidence and resilience are great, but only when they fit who you are. Toss out anything that feels forced.
- **Value connection:** True strength isn't in shutting people out—it's in building relationships that make you feel supported and seen.
- **Stay curious:** Growing as a person is about challenging old ideas, exploring new ones, and finding what helps you become the best version of yourself.

Breaking free from the manosphere is just step one. If we really want to challenge outdated ideas about masculinity, we've got to zoom out and see the bigger picture.

GIRLS AREN'T THE ENEMY

By now, we've unpacked how the manosphere twists masculinity into something narrow and harmful. But let's zoom out and talk about two big ideas: misogyny and feminism. These concepts are at the core of how society treats gender—and how we can all do better.

Misogyny: The Sneaky Side of Sexism

Let's start with the basics: misogyny is the dislike, contempt, or ingrained prejudice against women. It's sexism turned up a notch, where biases against women aren't just casual—they're deeply rooted in culture and sometimes even celebrated. And sure, it might sound dramatic, like the guy yelling slurs on a street corner or the villain in a movie sneering at women. But misogyny isn't always loud or obvious.

Sometimes, misogyny is quieter, subtle, even. It's the joke about "women drivers" that gets an awkward chuckle, or ignoring your female classmate's ideas during a project discussion. These smaller moments might feel harmless in the moment, but they're like those tiny rocks that get in your shoes—insignificant alone, but over time? They hurt. Every day, misogyny stacks up, creating a culture where women's talents and voices are undervalued. And that limits everyone.

To put it plainly: real strength doesn't come from putting others down. It comes from lifting everyone up.

Why Feminism Matters (Yes, Even for Guys)

Okay, let's get this out of the way: feminism isn't anti-men. It's not about guilting you for liking football, video games, or whatever else society labels as "manly." Feminism is about one thing—equality. It's the belief that everyone deserves the same rights and opportunities, regardless of gender.

So, why should this matter to you? Because feminism doesn't just help women—it helps *you*. Think about it: feminism pushes back against outdated stereotypes that say men can't cry, always have to be "the strong one," or shouldn't care about things like relationships and empathy. Those old rules? They're exhausting.

Here's what feminism isn't:

- It's not about erasing masculinity.
- It's not about blaming men for everything.
- It's not a membership club that requires you to burn all your "manly" interests.

Here's what it is:

- A movement that says you don't have to fit into a narrow definition of being a man.

- A chance to create a fairer world where respect and opportunity are the norms for everyone.

When you support feminism, you're not giving up anything. You're showing that you value fairness, growth, and respect—qualities that make you stronger, not weaker.

What You Can Do

But how do you take all this and make it part of your life without turning it into a chore? With a few surprisingly simple steps:

- **Start conversations:** Talk to the women in your life —your friends, sisters, teachers—and actually listen to their experiences. You'll gain perspectives that can shift how you see the world.
- **Learn the history:** Feminism isn't a new trend. It's been a long fight for equality, and understanding that history gives you the tools to recognize what still needs to change.
- **Be mindful online:** Before liking, sharing, or laughing at something, think about whether it punches down or reinforces stereotypes. Small choices add up.
- **Speak up:** When someone cracks a sexist joke or dismisses women, don't let it slide. A simple "That's not cool" can go a long way in setting the tone.
- **Be a supporter:** Being supportive does not ask for grand gestures—it's about showing up in small but meaningful ways. Support equality at home, at school, and online.

By embracing feminism, you're not only backing others but

giving yourself a shot at something better. A world where strength teams up with kindness, masculinity gets a modern upgrade, and everyone finally gets the respect they deserve.

You don't have to do it perfectly. Just start. Every step you take toward fairness and understanding makes a difference.

BEING STRONG AND KIND

Think of masculinity as a playlist. There are classic tracks—strength, independence, bravery—that never go out of style. But you're the DJ. You decide what gets turned up, what gets skipped, and which new tracks make the cut.

Don't let anyone fool you! Healthy masculinity is rooted in balance. It lets you express your emotions without fear of judgment. You're not weak for crying after a rough day or for telling a friend that you're proud of them. In fact, those moments of vulnerability make you stronger and deepen your connections. It's also about listening, validating others' feelings, and standing against behaviors that harm or belittle. Calling out disrespect doesn't make you less of a man; it makes you someone people trust and admire.

There's no one real definition of masculinity. The beauty of it is that you get to draw from the best traits, like resilience and confidence, while rejecting the toxic baggage. By shaping your own identity, you're proving that masculinity isn't about fitting into a rigid mold. It's about standing tall in your own truth.

That truth gets tested, sharpened, and shaped in the relationships that matter most. Time to zoom in on family, friends, and the people who help build the man you're becoming.

THREE
FRIENDS AND FAMILY REMIX

During your teen years, home starts feeling... different. It's not that your family suddenly becomes unbearable—though, yeah, some days they really test your limits. What's actually shifting is you. You're craving more space—time to think your own thoughts, make your own calls, or just exist without someone asking where you're going every five minutes.

As that need grows, your friends start to matter more. They get your humor without a full explanation, catch your references without a rewind, and make it easier to just be yourself without feeling like you have to perform or explain.

This change isn't only about who you'd rather hang out with—it's about figuring out who you are, what feels right, and how you want to show up in the world. That internal shift starts shaping everything around you.

And if you're feeling the tension, chances are it's showing up at home first. So that's where we're starting.

SAME CREW, NEW VIBES

Think of your family like a team on a road trip. Your parents are in the front seat, navigating and making the rules, while you're in the back seat, starting to wonder if you could drive the car yourself. Puberty is like hitting a weird stretch of the journey where the GPS glitches and everyone's a little cranky.

Suddenly, the whole vibe shifts. You're not trying to be difficult —you're just becoming your own person with your own ideas about how things should work. Meanwhile, your parents are still used to being the ones calling all the shots. The result? Everyone's bumping into each other as you all try to figure out this new dynamic.

The Push for Independence

So what does this new dynamic actually look like day to day? For starters, you probably don't want to be around your family as much. Hanging out with your mates feels way more fun, way more you. It's not that you've ditched your family—it's just that your world is getting bigger, and you're figuring out where you fit in it.

That's when the little arguments start piling up. Curfews feel outdated. Chores turn into battles. Screen time limits feel like a personal attack. Making weekend plans suddenly requires negotiations that feel like you're applying for a passport. You're not trying to stir up drama—you're just starting to have your own way of seeing things.

At the core of all the back-and-forth is your totally legit need for independence. Maybe that means experimenting with your style, setting your own boundaries, or just wanting to be the one who decides when it's time to unplug. All of that makes sense.

The tricky part is that while you're learning to step forward, your parents are trying to step back without feeling pushed out.

They've spent years managing the details—snacks, schedules, scraped knees—and now they're being asked to hand over the metaphorical keys. While they trust you, it's not easy for them to stop reaching for the brakes.

Still Your Crew

Even when they embarrass you in public or text "k" like it's a full sentence, your family is still part of your foundation. The arguments, the eye rolls, and the weird attempts at jokes don't cancel out the fact that these are the people who've been in your corner since day one.

Turns out, that's not just a nice idea. It's backed by actual science (nerd alert, but stay with me). Research shows that teens who feel supported at home tend to have higher self-esteem, stronger focus, and a way lower chance of spiraling into risky choices. They bounce back faster from stress, handle setbacks without losing their grip, and carry this quiet confidence that comes from knowing someone's in their corner, no matter what.

Ways to Stay Connected

You don't need to be inseparable; you can just make small choices that keep the bond strong. Try this:

- **Make one-on-one time:** Family time *as a unit* can feel... intense. But sneak in some dedicated one-on-one time with your parents or siblings. Think mini-quests: walk the dog together (if your dog is cool, obvs), dominate a board game tournament, or just... vent about your day over a snack. These tiny pockets of connection are surprisingly powerful.

- **Show love and appreciation:** Let your fam know you appreciate them, even if your default teen face is "mildly annoyed." Drop an "I love you" like it's no big deal, unleash a hug (if you're a hugger, no pressure), offer to help with chores *before* being asked (mind-blowing, I know), or even just scribble a quick "thanks for being you" note. Expressing gratitude and affection is a major bond-strengthening.
- **Join your family when they leave the house:** Family outings might not top your weekend wishlist, but try to tag along on family adventures. That random weekend trip your parents were weirdly excited about, a movie night with too much popcorn, or checking out that new burger spot? Might not sound like much now, but moments like those turn into memory checkpoints.
- **Agree on household responsibilities:** Helping out around the house might not be your dream gig, but this is where real-life skills are built. Showing up says, "Yeah, I've got this," without needing a speech. It also shifts the energy from "you live here rent-free" to "we're a team." Less nagging, more respect—a solid trade.

When you put even a little effort into keeping those relationships steady, you're not just being a "good son" or "responsible sibling." You're building a support system that'll have your back when things get chaotic, confusing, or flat-out hard.

Still, not every part of you fits neatly into family life. Some parts are just starting to take shape—quirks, moods, ideas—and that's where friendship takes over.

WHY YOUR CREW BECOMES YOUR TRIBE

Friends become the space where you can test-drive the new version of yourself. Back when you were younger, friendship was simple. If someone shared their snacks, let you pick the game, or lived close by, that was enough. It was more about fun than connection—someone to laugh with, run around with, and just keep things easy.

But now, what you need from your crew starts to shift. It's not just about having someone to hang out with—it's about being around people who actually get you. The ones who notice when you're quiet and don't make it weird. The ones who respect your interests, even if they're not into the same stuff. The ones who don't bail just because you're having an off day.

Not every friendship makes that jump. Some people drift, and some change in ways that don't match where you're headed. That's not drama—it's just growth. What matters are the ones who keep pace with you, show up when it counts, and let you be fully yourself without needing to explain.

Why Friends Feel Like Everything

There's actually a reason your friendships start to feel way more intense during your teen years—and it's not just hormones or drama. As puberty kicks in, the parts of your brain that deal with social connection, emotional safety, and peer belonging start firing up like never before. That's why your friends' opinions matter more, why rejection stings harder, and why finding people who really get you feels less like a bonus and more like a need.

It's not just about fitting in. Your brain is learning how to be part of a world that's bigger than your family. Early friendships are practice for everything that comes next—figuring out trust, support, loyalty, and even conflict. And researchers have found that people who build strong, honest friendships as teens tend to carry those skills into the rest of their lives. They're better at handling stress, building close relationships, and feeling grounded in who they are.

So if your friendships feel bigger, louder, and more intense than ever? That's because they actually are.

How to Spot Your Real Friends (MVPs)

So, how do you figure out who is actually a friend versus someone you just hang with sometimes? Here's the thing—popularity and follower counts mean absolutely nothing when it comes to real friendship. What matters is finding people who show up for you in ways that actually count:

1. **They root for you:** A real friend will cheer you on when you score the winning point, bomb a test (but vow to do better), or finally gather the courage to talk to your crush. It is not about competition; it is about celebration.
2. **They respect your boundaries:** If you are feeling overwhelmed and need downtime, they do not make you feel guilty. If you say, "Nah, I'm not into that," they let it go instead of poking. Respect is non-negotiable.
3. **They let you be weird:** Everyone has quirks—maybe you love reorganizing your desk drawers when you are stressed, or you have an odd fascination with detective shows. A true friend does not just put up with your quirks; they appreciate them.
4. **They stick around even when it's messy:** Life can get hectic—family issues, breakups, or just feeling stuck in a funk. A genuine friend does not vanish when things get complicated.

Ironically, the best friendships often pop up when you are not hunting for them. They form because of a shared sense of humor or mutual respect, and before you know it, you have got a person you can call at 2 a.m. for advice on literally anything.

Friendship Hacks: Level Up Your Bond

Friendships don't run on autopilot. They need energy, just like your phone needs a charge. If you leave them on 1%, always assuming they'll just power through, things start to glitch. Here's how to keep the battery full without burning out:

- **Show up IRL:** Sure, online chats are great, but nothing beats hanging out in real life. Whether it's skateboarding, a movie night, or just chilling in the backyard, being present matters.
- **Master real talk mode:** Surface-level convos are fine, but being honest and open is what makes a friendship epic. Got a problem? Share it. Your friend's going through a rough patch? Be all ears.
- **Empathy power-up:** Life gets messy sometimes. Understanding your friend's perspective, even when you don't agree, can turn arguments into growth moments.

Friendships will give you some of the best moments and memories, but they also shape how you see yourself, how you show up, and what risks you're willing to take. That kind of influence can build you up or push you somewhere you're not ready—or don't want—to go.

UNDERSTANDING PEER PRESSURE

Before we get into peer pressure, let's clear up what *peers* actually are. Your peers are people who are around your age, going through the same general stage of life. They're your classmates, teammates, neighbors, or anyone else who gets what it's like to be where you are right now. Basically, they're the people you relate to because you're growing through the same stuff.

When Peer Pressure Is a Good Thing

Let's drop the idea that peer pressure is always some evil force trying to ruin your life. Because believe it or not, positive peer pressure is real, and when it shows up, it can be a game-changer.

Think about the friend who pushes you to try out for the basketball team, even though you were nervous. Or the one who calls you out (in a good way) when you're slacking on schoolwork. Or that one group of friends who actually make studying a kind of fun. Sometimes, your crew sees potential in you that you haven't noticed yet, and gives you the nudge you didn't know you needed.

When Peer Pressure Turns Toxic

Of course, not all peer pressure comes from a good place. Sometimes, the push from your peers doesn't feel supportive at all—it feels off. Like a plot twist you didn't sign up for.

It doesn't always look like a group yelling, "Come on, do it!" Sometimes it's subtle. A friend might tease you for not ditching class. Someone might roll their eyes because you won't break a rule. You end up in a situation that feels wrong, but you go along with it because you don't want to seem lame, soft, or left out.

That's the kind of pressure that can mess with your gut.

Learning to spot it—and figuring out how to hold your line—is what keeps you from getting dragged into choices that don't feel like you. It's not about being perfect. It's about knowing when something crosses a line and trusting yourself enough to say, "Nah, I'm good."

How to Keep Your Cool When Pressured

- **Trust your gut:** That weird, twisty feeling in your stomach? It's your brain's way of saying, "Something's off." If a situation makes you feel tense, anxious, or just not like yourself, don't ignore it. You don't need a perfect excuse to walk away—discomfort is reason enough.
- **Play it forward:** Before you go along with something, ask yourself, *"If this showed up on a highlight reel of my life, would I feel proud or cringe?"* That one question can save you from regret. If the answer's no, it's okay to say no now, even if it means standing out.
- **Hold the line:** Saying "Nah, I'm good" doesn't need to come with an angry speech or a dramatic exit. Keep it simple. Keep it calm. People respect confidence more than explanations.
- **Redirect the vibe:** A lot of pressure comes from boredom. The group wants energy, not necessarily trouble. Offer an alternative that still sounds fun: grab snacks, hit a basketball court, binge something dumb on YouTube.

Real friends do not bail on you if you set a boundary. They might give you a playful eye roll, but they will move on. If someone keeps pushing after you have clearly said no, it is probably time to reevaluate that relationship.

FROM INNER CIRCLES TO HEART CIRCLES

You've figured out the balancing act—keeping your family in the loop without feeling like a kid, building friendships that actually support you, and dodging the kind of peer pressure that makes you second-guess yourself. Let's jump into the first quiz and see what you've locked in.

QUIZ: GROWING PAINS AND POWER-UPS

Go through each question and pick the answer you think is correct. No rush, no pressure. Just check what you know.

1. **What actually flips the puberty "on" switch in your body?**
    a. The vocal cords stretch
    b. The hypothalamus signals the pituitary gland
    c. The muscles start growing on their own
2. **Which hormone runs the show during male puberty?**
    a. Dopamine
    b. Estrogen
    c. Testosterone
3. **Why might you suddenly feel awkward in your body during puberty?**
    a. You're shrinking
    b. Your body is growing unevenly and fast
    c. You're dehydrated
4. **Why do wet dreams happen?**
    a. Your body is adjusting to new physical abilities
    b. You're not getting enough sleep
    c. It means something is wrong
5. **What's a good example of an emotional change during puberty?**
    a. Liking pizza more than before
    b. Laughing at the same meme all day
    c. Feeling more intense moods than usual
6. **What's the problem with toxic masculinity?**
    a. It tells you to always show emotions

b. It expects guys to hide emotions and act tough all the time
c. It teaches respect and communication

7. **What's one way to spot a toxic message online about being a man?**
   a. It talks about sharing emotions
   b. It blames women for men's problems
   c. It encourages friendships
8. **What does feminism actually stand for?**
   a. Making things harder for boys
   b. Giving everyone equal rights and respect
   c. Ending sports

The answers are at the back of the book—so no peeking.

PART TWO
DATING, SEX, AND RESPECT

FOUR
CRUSHES AND DATING

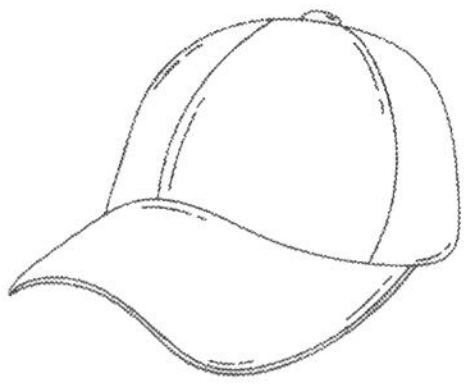

One minute you're just doing your thing, and then someone says something funny, posts a new pic, or walks past you in the hallway—and your brain short-circuits. You start thinking about them for no real reason. You check their profile once. Then again. And now every little thing—walking to class, replying to a DM, picking the right hoodie—feels like it somehow matters more than it should.

That's how it kicks off.

What happens after that depends on how things play out, but there's a pattern most people hit, whether it's a full-on crush, a quick situationship, or something in between. Let's break down the stages.

STAGE ONE: TESTING THE VIBE

It usually kicks off with something low-key—a blurry half-face, a "hey" with zero punctuation, or maybe a goofy filter just to test the waters. Feels casual, but that snap is doing more than it looks. It's quietly asking, *"I think you're cool. Are you feeling this too?"*

Even if it seems chill on the outside, sending that first message takes guts. Whether it's a one-word DM or a snap that vanishes in three seconds, you're still putting yourself out there. That's not nothing.

No one's locked in yet. You might be snapping one person, or bouncing between a few convos just to see who brings something better than "wyd." That's not shady—it's just how Stage One works. It's the vibe check stage.

Tips for Stage One

- **Be authentic:** If you're into gaming, why not send a screenshot of your latest high score? Love art? Share a sneak peek of your newest doodle.
- **Respect privacy:** Sharing without permission is a huge no-no. If they send a private snap, don't screenshot or share, ever. That matters, especially early on.
- **Avoid cling mode:** A few thoughtful snaps will always carry more meaning than constant check-ins. Sure, keeping a snap streak might look cool on your profile, but quality always beats quantity.

Sometimes it clicks. Sometimes it doesn't. You might get a dry reply, a late one, or none at all. That's not a fail—it's just a signal to move on. Stage One is all about testing the waters, not trying to win anyone over.

But if you notice you're actually hoping their name lights up your screen because you want to talk? Yeah, that means you're sliding into Stage Two.

STAGE TWO: LOW-KEY LIKING

You're not just snapping to keep a streak alive or reacting to stories with the usual fire emoji. Now it's more like, "Did you survive math?" or "Still up?"—small stuff that means you actually want to know.

The vibe's still casual, but it's got more warmth now. You've got an inside joke now. Maybe a weird nickname. There's a filter you both keep using for no reason except that it makes you both laugh. You're texting more often—sometimes late—and whether you admit it or not, you're starting to notice how long they take to reply. You read into it. You care.

Still, Stage Two's early game. It's fun, yeah—but also a little shaky. You might wonder if they're talking to other people, or if you're the only one catching feelings. That's normal. This part's not about racing ahead. It's about seeing what kind of connection this is.

Handling Stage Two

- **Keep it chill:** Not every message needs to be deep or clever. Let the conversation breathe. If it's a real connection, it won't need constant effort to stay alive.
- **Open up a little:** You don't have to spill your life story, but sharing what you're into—or even what's been tough lately—can help the other person see more of the real you. That's where actual closeness starts.
- **Protect your time:** If you're slammed with homework, sports, or just need a break, say so. A quick "Can't talk now—catch you later" is honest and mature.
- **Stay curious:** Ask real questions. Notice how they

respond. Are they kind? Do they listen? Do your values match? That tells you more than any "wyd" ever will.

When the convo stops feeling like something you're *starting* and more like something neither of you wants to end—that's when you know Stage Three's on the horizon.

STAGE THREE: SPEAKING IRL

At some point, the screen just stops being enough. The chats are solid, the replies are fast, the jokes are inside—but you're still wondering what they're like in person. That's the signal. When texting isn't cutting it and you catch yourself wishing you were actually with them instead of just talking about being with them, you're stepping into Stage Three.

Snaps feel safe. Real life? Not so much. Suddenly, you're thinking about what to wear, where to stand, whether your breath is weird, and what to do with your hands. Chill. Everyone goes through it. It just means this matters more now.

The First Hangout

Meeting up doesn't have to be a big deal or carry the label of an official date—unless you both decide to call it that—it's just two people showing up, hoodie on, nerves buzzing, maybe sipping a half-finished iced tea, trying to see if the vibe that worked online still makes sense in real life.

What are the options?

- **Go with the crew:** Invite them to hang out with your other friends—mall, movies, food court. Low pressure.

You can talk when it feels right, and they get to see what you're like in your natural habitat.
    - Keep in mind that your squad might be super relaxed, but this person's still new to the vibe. Don't forget to include them.
- **Make it active:** Not feeling the group thing? Try something where there's something to do while you talk. Mini golf, arcade, even walking through a park, or grabbing snacks from a corner store, can take the edge off.
- **Keep it public:** Whatever the plan, make sure it's somewhere neutral and public. It helps keep things comfortable and safe for both of you.

Hacks for Stage Three

Meeting someone you like but don't really know can make you feel shy or socially awkward. That's normal. There might be weird silences, or you might talk too fast, or not at all.

Instead of trying to fill every silence with small talk, try something easy that takes the pressure off. A few solid fallbacks:

- "What song do you have on loop right now?"
- "You get one free pass to skip any school subject forever. Which one?"
- "What's your go-to order at [insert popular local fast food spot]?"
- "Which game or show could you play/watch forever without getting bored?"
- "If you had to trade lives with a character from any movie or series, who would it be?"

Questions like these show personality and open the door to real conversation without making it feel like an interview.

Is This Something?

After you've hung out—even just once—something shifts. The way you text changes. You remember what they say. You hear their voice when you read their replies. You care more—even if you don't say it out loud.

You start paying closer attention. Like, *real* attention. How they act around other people. Whether they laugh at your dumbest joke. If they treat people with respect when no one's watching. That's the stuff that starts to matter.

And yeah, somewhere in all of that, the question shows up: *Is this actually a thing?*

You don't need to figure it out right away. Stage Three isn't about rushing into labels—it's about watching the vibe grow. Letting it prove itself. The easy mistake here? Getting caught up in the excitement and trying to skip ahead. Don't.

Take your time. Enjoy the weird, exciting, slightly awkward energy of it all. This stage only happens once with each person, and it's where you learn the most about them *and* yourself.

So, how do you know Stage Four's getting close?

- You actually miss them, *not* just the streak or the messages. Them.
- You start thinking about how your choices affect them.
- You catch yourself wanting to bring them into your world—your music, your friends, your weekend plans.
- You're not just wondering if *they* like *you* anymore. You're asking if *this* feels right for *you*.

If the answer is yes—and it feels real, not rushed—you're heading into something more official.

STAGE FOUR: EXCLUSIVE OR NOT EXCLUSIVE?

This is where things start to take shape—even if you haven't spelled it out. You're not just talking, not casually flirting with other people, and not wondering if this means something. The connection's there, and it's starting to feel like a choice—even without a label.

You might not have said the words "we're exclusive," but the way you act already says it. You text more without thinking about who texts first. You check in because you want to. You make plans that feel natural, not like a big deal. There's trust building, and now it actually matters when one of you goes quiet.

That's the shift. You stop thinking just for yourself and start considering how your choices land on someone else. What you do affects them. What they do hits you, too. That's when it stops being just a vibe and starts being something real.

Balancing "Us Time" and "You Time"

One of the fastest ways to mess up a new relationship? Dropping everything else to be with them. Hanging out 24/7 might seem like the move, but if you start ghosting your group chat, bailing on plans, or skipping the stuff you usually love just to stay "available," it stops being fun—and starts feeling off.

Bringing someone new into your life can shift the whole balance. Your friends are used to having you around, and now you're splitting your time. Even when you're happy with your crush, you might catch yourself wondering what the boys are doing without you. You feel the pull in both directions. That's normal.

So what do you do?

- **Keep your friendships alive:** You don't have to spend equal time everywhere, but don't vanish either. Let your crew know they still matter.
- **Hold onto your own stuff:** Whether it's skating, music, solo time, or whatever keeps your brain sane, don't trade it for couple time 100% of the time.
- **Find your rhythm:** Maybe your crush likes texting all day. Maybe you don't. That's fine—as long as you're real about it.

Some people think dating means non-stop texting, holding hands every chance you get, and posting couple selfies on blast. Hey, if you're both into that? Cool. Just don't assume everyone is.

If the person you're seeing isn't into public affection, respect that. If you're ready for more closeness—like hugs, hand-holding, or kissing—ask. Don't guess. Don't push. Consent isn't just for the big stuff—it's about all the small moments too.

Also, not every solid relationship is all about being physical. Some people show they care by remembering what you said, grabbing your favorite drink, or texting you good luck before something big. That kind of effort counts just as much.

When Issues Come Up

Even the match-made-in-heaven couples argue. Maybe you're both stressed about a test, or you get jealous because they liked someone else's post a little too eagerly. Conflict is normal, but how you handle it defines your relationship's vibe.

- **Stay respectful:** No name-calling, no belittling. You can be mad without being mean.

- **Listen:** Let them explain their side before you jump in with "You're wrong!"
- **Apologize when needed:** If you messed up, own it. A sincere "I'm sorry" goes a long way.

Yeah, it's work sometimes. Real relationships aren't just vibes and playlists. They take effort. You have to show up even when it's not fun or convenient.

But when do you get it right? When does it actually feel like both of you are on the same team? It starts to feel legit. The thing is, not every connection works that way, and some can do more harm than good.

Recognizing Toxic Red Flags

If your partner starts acting in ways that feel off—not just annoying, but straight-up toxic—that's a whole different situation. Watch out for stuff like:

- **Trying to control you:** They demand your phone password or want updates on everyone you text, all the time.
- **Cutting you off:** They push you to ditch your friends and act like it's only okay to hang out with them.
- **Constant put-downs:** They make fun of your clothes, your interests, or even your body—and it doesn't feel like joking.
- **Guilt trips and threats:** They say stuff like, "If you really loved me, you'd do this," or, "I'll hurt myself if you leave."

None of that is normal. None of it is okay. You don't need

permission to walk away. If someone's messing with your mental or emotional health, that's more than enough reason to bounce.

STAGE FIVE: THE ICK

Sometimes everything clicks—and sometimes, out of the blue, you just get the ick. Suddenly, the way they chew their gum or the jokes they repeat ten times start making your skin crawl. It might not even be something they *did* wrong—it's just a gut feeling that you're not into them anymore. The ick can be mild—like a quick "ugh" that passes—or it can be so strong you want to bail immediately.

Don't beat yourself up if it happens. Attraction can be weirdly unpredictable. Still, if you're at Stage Four and catch a full-on ick, it's probably time to talk it out or reconsider the relationship. For some couples, it's just a phase. For others, it's a sign this relationship has run its course.

Breaking Up With Respect

Now, let's say you've decided it's time to move on. Breaking up is never fun, but it doesn't have to be messy either. Here's how to end things in a way that keeps your integrity (and your partner's dignity) intact:

- **Be honest, not harsh:** Skip the clichés like "It's not you, it's me," and explain your feelings clearly and calmly. Keep it real but kind—there's no need to list every grievance.
- **Do it face-to-face:** No ghosting, no breakup texts. Unless it's absolutely unsafe to meet in person, having the conversation face-to-face shows maturity and respect.

- **Be ready for emotions:** Your partner might feel hurt, angry, or even confused. That's normal. Be patient, but stand your ground—you don't owe anyone a relationship.

Yes, breakups can feel like the end of the world, especially your first serious one. But spoiler alert: you *will* survive. Lean on friends, family, or a trusted adult if you're really struggling. Practice self-care —play that game you love, watch your comfort show, or pick up a new hobby. Eventually, you'll look back and see how much you grew from the experience. Sometimes, heartbreak is a weirdly effective teacher.

THE REAL ADVENTURE IS GETTING TO KNOW YOURSELF

You've seen that romance isn't just some side quest in your teen life —it's part of your actual story. Whether you're swapping memes, catching feelings, going on first dates, or dealing with the awkward "umm, what are we?" moments, every stage teaches you something new, not just about other people, but about *you*.

You don't need to be smooth, perfect, or 100% sure of what you're doing. You just need to be real. The more honest you are—with your feelings, your boundaries, your hopes, your no-thanks—the easier it becomes to spot what works and what doesn't. That's the real skill: learning to listen to yourself, even when everything around you is loud.

If you've been paying attention, noticing what feels right and what doesn't, you've already gathered the tools you need. Now let's put them to work in Sex 101.

FIVE
SEX 101

You've probably already heard about sex from friends, the internet, jokes, or health classes. Some of it might've been funny, some uncomfortable, and most probably left you with more questions than answers.

This is your first step into understanding sex. Not the "birds and the bees," not locker room myths, and not vague warnings—just clear information.

YOUR OWN PRIVATE THING

Before you even think about intimacy with someone else, there's a good chance you'll explore the solo route first: masturbation.

This is one of those words people avoid like Voldemort, but what is it exactly? Masturbation is when you touch your own genitals for pleasure, often leading to orgasm. It's a private way to figure out what feels good—no risk of pregnancy, no STIs, and no one else involved. Just you, your body, and a little curiosity.

Some guys do it often, some rarely, and some never. Every

version is normal. If you're curious, it helps to find a quiet moment when you won't get walked in on and just see what feels right for you; if it's not your thing, no problem. This isn't a test you pass or a habit you need to pick up.

The Science of Figuring You Out

A little one-on-one time with yourself also has some science-backed benefits. Puberty can ramp up testosterone fast—fueling your sex drive, pumping up your energy, and sometimes leaving you feeling restless or on edge. While masturbation doesn't lower those hormone levels, it *does* give your system a way to release that built-up tension and channel the intensity in a way that's private, safe, and completely normal.

Meanwhile, your brain is doing its part too. Orgasm triggers the release of dopamine and endorphins—those feel-good chemicals that can boost your mood, help you relax, and even make it easier to sleep.

On top of that, you're learning what feels good, what doesn't, and how your body reacts—all without the pressure of anyone else being involved. That kind of awareness lays the groundwork for boundaries, clear communication, and healthier relationships later on.

Now, since there are still some weird myths hanging around, let's clear a few of those up:

- **"It's something to be ashamed of or feel guilty about."**
  - **Definitely not:** Masturbation is a healthy, safe, and private way to explore your body. There's nothing to feel guilty or embarrassed about. It's your body, your rules, and your experience.

- **"Doing it too much will make you go bald, grow hair on your palms, or mess up your eyesight."**
    - **Nope:** There is absolutely no scientific connection between touching yourself and losing your hair, needing glasses, or any other weird physical symptom. Your hairline, your eyesight, and your overall physical health are completely safe.
- **"Only lonely guys do it, or it means you can't get a girlfriend/partner."**
    - **Nah:** Even people in happy relationships do it. Masturbating is not a sign you're a loner or undesirable.
- **"You can get addicted to it."**
    - **Could you overdo it? Maybe:** For the vast, vast majority of people, masturbation is just a normal, healthy part of life that can be easily managed. If you ever feel like it's controlling you or stopping you from doing other important things, that's a sign to talk to a trusted adult or counselor.

WHAT IS SEXUAL ATTRACTION?

As your body changes and you grow, you'll also start noticing new kinds of pulls toward other people.

For a lot of guys, these first real feelings of sexual attraction tend to kick in around mid-puberty—between the ages of 10 and 14—when hormone levels really start to surge. But it can also happen earlier or later.

Who you're attracted to can vary, too:

- Some guys are into girls (straight)

- Some are into guys (gay)
- Some are into both (bi)
- Some don't really feel that sexual pull toward anyone (asexual)
- And some only feel it after building a strong emotional connection (demisexual)

Attraction looks and feels different for everyone, and it doesn't always make sense at first. That's part of figuring yourself out.

What It Feels Like

There's a split second when you see someone, and suddenly you feel a different kind of buzz. Not just thinking, "Yeah, they're cool," like you would about a game or a new pair of sneakers.

Your brain and body sync up in a way that feels more intense than just wanting to hang out. There's curiosity, maybe nerves, and a pull that's hard to explain.

The wild part? It's not your heart doing some rom-com thing—it's your brain on overdrive, firing off a cocktail of chemicals that hit fast and hard:

- **Dopamine** (the "this feels amazing" hormone),
- **Adrenaline** (cue sweaty palms and racing heart),
- **Oxytocin** (a.k.a. the bonding chemical).

Even if you barely know the person, that internal rush can feel huge, leaving you nervous, curious, or totally caught off guard.

Why You Notice

So, what flips that internal switch? It depends. What makes one guy's head turn might not even register for another. But generally, your brain is picking up on a few key signals:

- **Physical appeal:** Maybe it's their smile, their voice, or the way they move. Your brain naturally picks up on traits that signal confidence, health, or compatibility.
- **Emotional connection:** Some people are more drawn to personality over looks. Maybe it's the way they make you laugh, how they get your sense of humor, or how easy it is to talk to them.
- **Shared experiences:** The more time you spend with someone, the stronger the attraction can grow. Familiarity and comfort build connection, and suddenly, that person you never noticed before? Now they're on your mind.

This is your brain just flagging someone as "potential." It doesn't mean you have to act on it, chase it, or turn it into something more. You're allowed to pause, be curious, or let it pass. The important thing is knowing it's yours and you get to decide what it means.

WHAT YOU NEED TO KNOW BEFORE YOU HAVE SEX

Textbooks will tell you that sex is all about making babies, sure, but there's way more happening under the surface. Before we dive into the juicy details in the next chapter, here are a few things that don't always get said out loud:

Not Everyone Talks About It the Same Way

People grow up with very different messages about sex. Some families are open and chill about it. Others act like the word itself is off-limits. Culture, religion, school, and even friend groups all shape how much someone knows.

Understanding this matters. It allows you to respect the other person's values and recognize that access to real information isn't equal for everyone. What seems obvious to you might be brand new to someone else.

That means when you're talking to someone else about sex, they might be coming from a totally different place. Be kind and honest.

It's a Two-Person Experience

Sex at its best is something two people want, enjoy, and feel good about. That means watching how your partner reacts, checking in with a quick "you good?" and listening to the answer.

Learning to give pleasure, not just chase your own, is what turns the physical into something more. Being a good partner means showing up with care.

Sex and the Law

This part's serious. Sex has legal boundaries, and they matter more than most people think. You need to be the legal age—usually between 16 and 18—to even agree to sex.

Consent is also non-negotiable. We'll break that down fully in a couple of chapters, but for now, remember: Consent is the Golden Rule of every healthy sexual experience. It's a constant agreement that can change at any time. Both people have to be fully into it, aware, and free to say no without pressure.

Getting this wrong has real consequences, like criminal charges. You don't need all the answers right now, but understanding this is step one toward doing it right.

WHO, WHEN, AND HOW SOON?

You're probably thinking, "Okay, I get all of this. But how do I know if I'm *ready* for sex?" First, take a deep breath. Just because people say everyone's "doing it" doesn't mean it's true. A lot of teens choose to wait, even if they don't say it out loud.

Across the world, people start at different times. In countries like Sweden and Denmark, the average age for first-time sex is around 16. In the U.S., New Zealand, and Australia, it's closer to 17 or 18. Meanwhile, in places like India, Malaysia, Egypt, and Indonesia, many people wait until their 20s or even until marriage.

Ready or Not?

To choose, you need to know where you are mentally, emotionally, and physically. Here's a quick gut check:

- Do you actually want this, or are you just trying not to be the last one?
- Are you okay with how your body's changing and how you feel in it?
- Would you feel solid afterward, or second-guess it the next day?
- Are you and your partner on the same page, for real, not just assuming?

If any part of you is hesitating, that's self-awareness. If your reason for considering sex sounds like:

- "Everyone else is doing it."
- "I just want to get it over with."
- "They'll leave if I don't."
- "I'll finally feel older."

Then, it's probably not the right time.

You're the boss. No one else gets to decide when you're ready to hit that next level. Stay true to what feels right for you.

READY FOR WHAT'S NEXT?

You've unpacked what sex is, how attraction works, and how to tell if you're truly ready for physical intimacy. That's a lot to take in, but it's crucial groundwork.

Now, if you're wondering what actually happens when things get physical—like, step-by-step, the whole deal—and how to keep it safe and good, then let's keep going. We're switching gears from just talking about it to what happens in real life when you decide to go there.

SIX
THE REAL SEX TALK

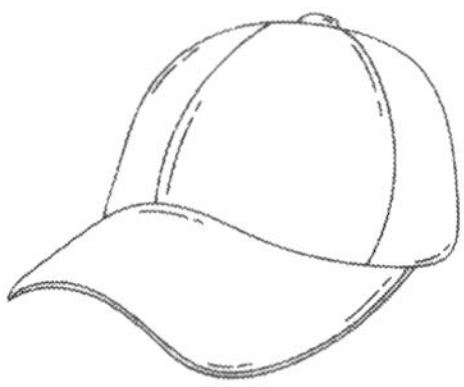

You've already thought through the why, the when, and whether you're even ready. Now it's time to talk about what happens when you go from thinking to doing.

This isn't just about where body parts go; it's about tuning in, slowing down, and making the whole thing feel good for both of you. Whether you're curious, about to have your first experience, or just want to get better at it, the more you understand, the better it gets.

Let's get into what makes sex safe, real, and enjoyable.

SETTING THE STAGE

You've probably heard the word *foreplay* and may have wondered what the big deal is. If sex were a video game, foreplay would be all the cool stuff that happens before the final boss fight—and skipping it is like trying to beat the game on level one. No build-up, no momentum, and no chance you're actually ready.

Foreplay includes everything physical and emotional that happens before intercourse—kissing, touching, teasing, and flirting.

It's where connection builds, nerves settle, and excitement grows. And here's what a lot of guys miss: this isn't just killing time or being "nice." It's what makes the entire experience better for *both* people.

Your body doesn't just flip into arousal mode—and neither does the other person's. It takes time to warm up: blood flow increases, nerves relax, and natural lubrication kicks in. For girls especially, that warm-up process usually takes longer—about 20 minutes on average. If you skip it, things can feel rushed, uncomfortable, or just off. Like trying to microwave a frozen pizza in 30 seconds and being surprised it's still cold in the middle.

Being good at foreplay is kind of like having a cheat code for connection. You don't need tons of experience; you just need to pay attention. Be curious, respectful, and in tune. The guys who skip this part are usually the ones left wondering why things feel awkward, why the other person doesn't seem into it, or why the moment falls flat.

So what does foreplay actually look like in real life? Here's what it can include:

- **Kissing and touching:** Soft, slow, intense, playful–pretty much anything goes. Kissing is often the starting point, and a good kiss? That's like a special connection between two people who just click.
- **Erogenous zone check-in:** Basically, the parts of your body that are pleasure sensitive. And it's not just the obvious spots–there are definitely hidden gems all over (we'll get to those).
- **Oral stimulation:** Using your mouth, lips, and tongue in ways that make things feel even closer and more personal.
- **Teasing and flirting:** Sometimes, you don't even

need to touch. A playful comment, or even just laughing together, can be foreplay in itself, believe it or not.

Pleasure Zones

So, you're ready to dive into the moment, now what? This is where knowing your body—and tuning in to your partner's—really pays off.

This part of sex isn't just about going straight for the obvious. Certain areas are wired for pleasure, packed with nerve endings that react to touch, pressure, and temperature in ways that can dial up the intensity.

Let's take a quick look:

- **Lips and mouth:** Kissing might seem basic, but done right, it's anything but. It can start slow or playful and turn into something intense fast.
- **Neck and ears:** Soft kisses, whispers, or even just warm breath on the skin can create a big reaction. This area is packed with nerve endings, so don't underestimate it.
- **Chest and nipples:** Most people associate nipple sensitivity with girls, but guys have nerve endings there too. A little teasing, licking, or pressure can surprise you in a good way.
- **Inner thighs:** Touching or kissing the sensitive skin on inner thighs can get your brain and body hyped before anything even happens.
- **Genitals:** Obvious, yes—but rushing this part is a rookie move. For guys, the underside of the penis (called the frenulum) is especially sensitive. For someone with a vulva, the clitoris is the nerve center—literally. It has

over 8,000 nerve endings, more than any other part of the human body.

And check out these underrated spots:

- **Lower back:** A slow touch here can send tingles all the way down.
- **Wrists and palms:** Lightly kissing or tracing fingers on wrists? Surprisingly good.
- **Behind the knees:** Another spot people often forget about that's surprisingly sensitive.
- **Scalp and hairline:** Ever had someone run their fingers through your hair? Feels really good, right? That's because your scalp is full of nerve endings.

Not every zone works the same for everyone. What one person loves, another might not feel much from—and that's totally normal. The goal isn't to master a checklist. It's to pay attention, try things out, and notice how they respond. That's what makes intimacy feel real, not just physical.

When the lead-up is based on connection and curiosity, moving into intercourse becomes more natural.

INTERCOURSE

For a lot of people, when they hear the word *sex*, they immediately think it means penis-in-vagina intercourse. And yeah, that's a common part of it—but it's far from the whole story.

So, what does intercourse involve? Let's break down the main types:

- **Vaginal sex:** Is when a penis goes into a vagina. Yeah, it might sound like a health class definition, but there's much more going on than just body parts aligning. When someone with a vagina becomes aroused, their body prepares for penetration through natural lubrication and by relaxing and expanding the vaginal muscles. If they feel rushed or uncomfortable, these muscles can tense, making penetration feel difficult or painful. That's why taking your time, ensuring your partner feels good and safe, and communicating openly about what feels right makes all the difference.
- **Anal sex:** The anus is highly sensitive due to a dense concentration of nerve endings, which is why some people find anal play pleasurable. BUT (and this is a big but—literally), the anus doesn't self-lubricate. That means lube is non-negotiable. Going slow, checking in with your partner, and using a lubricant that works with condoms are all musts to avoid discomfort or injury. Also, the muscles in this area require relaxation; any forcing can cause harm.
- **Oral sex:** This one involves using your mouth, lips, and tongue to stimulate your partner's genitals. And yeah, it 100% counts as sex. Some people use it as a way to build up to other stuff, and for others, it's the main focus. Either way, it can be super intimate.

Every sex life is unique. Not every experience has to involve penetration to be real or feel intimate. The true goal is for both of you to get something good out of it, not just follow some script you read online.

When that trust lines up with physical pleasure—and both of

you are fully into it—you might reach that intense, full-body high "whoa" moment. This is what we call an orgasm.

THE "WHOA" MOMENT

Orgasms can be intense, amazing, confusing, or all of the above. They're not the whole point of sex, but they are part of what makes intimacy feel powerful. Still, when people treat them like the goal or stress about making one happen, it takes away from the mutual enjoyment.

Some people climax easily, while others need more time or different kinds of touch. Some don't focus on it at all. There's no right or wrong pace, and no one owes anyone a "perfect" result. The real win is feeling safe, seen, and in sync with the other person.

What's Happening in Your Body?

When you're sexually aroused, your brain kicks into gear. Chemicals like dopamine and oxytocin are released, creating a rush of warmth, closeness, and pleasure. Blood flow increases, breathing changes, and muscles tense—and when orgasm hits, your body lets go of all that pressure in a wave of contractions and release.

- **For people with a penis:** Orgasm usually happens right when you ejaculate (when fluid comes out). This is a reflex response to intense sexual stimulation.
- **For people with a vulva:** Orgasm often comes from clitoral stimulation and may involve rhythmic muscle contractions, flushed skin, or deep relaxation. It's not always visible or obvious from thc outside, and it doesn't always happen the same way twice.

Everybody reacts differently, and what works for one person won't always work for another. That's why tuning in, asking, and exploring with care matters more than any other move.

FINAL TOUCHES TO KEEP IN MIND

Once you've got the basics down, there are still a few non-negotiables to lock in:

- **Lube = Level up:** When there's not enough natural lubrication during sex, the skin can rub together in ways that feel uncomfortable or even painful. That extra friction can cause tiny skin tears, which not only hurt but also make it easier to pass STIs and increase the chance of a condom breaking. There are two main types:
    - **Water-based lubes:** Safe with all types of condoms and sex toys, making them a versatile choice.
    - **Silicone-based lubes:** Last longer, but can degrade silicone sex toys.
- **Bodies are just...weird:** Human bodies are complex, and sexual encounters can involve unexpected moments. Expect weird noises, random pauses, or even a surprise leg cramp. Best move? Laugh it off, talk it out, and keep going. It's human and totally normal. Don't let minor quirks throw you off or make you self-conscious.
- **Aftercare:** Sex doesn't just end when the physical act does. Aftercare involves checking in with each other emotionally and physically. This could mean cuddling, talking, sharing a snack, or simply ensuring both of you feel comfortable and connected. It's about respecting

each other's feelings and wrapping up the experience positively.

- **Hygiene matters:** A wash before and after sex can prevent infections. For penis, retracting the foreskin (if uncircumcised) and cleaning underneath is important. Good hygiene shows respect for yourself and your partner.

And since getting that close with someone can have real-world consequences, it's time we talk about keeping things safe and making smart moves.

CONTRACEPTION AND PROTECTION

If you're having sex, protection isn't something to "figure out later." It's a right-now responsibility. Contraception helps prevent unplanned pregnancy, and using it right can also lower your chances of getting a sexually transmitted infection (STI). Whether things are planned or spontaneous, protection means less stress, fewer regrets, and more respect for yourself and others.

What Are Your Options?

Contraceptive methods are designed to prevent pregnancy. Some, like condoms, also help protect against STIs—but not all. Here's what each option does and how to use it right:

- **Condoms:** The only single method that protects against both pregnancy and most STIs. They catch semen during ejaculation. With perfect use, they're about 98% effective at preventing pregnancy—but with typical use, they're closer to 87%. Condoms are available without a prescription and work instantly once they're on.

- **The right way to use one:**
    - Open the package carefully—no teeth, no scissors.
    - Pinch the tip to leave space for semen.
    - Roll it down all the way on an erect penis.
    - After ejaculation, hold the base while pulling out.
    - Wrap it in tissue and toss it—never flush.
    - Never double up. Using two condoms at once actually increases the chance of tearing.
    - Store them in a cool, dry place (not your wallet), and always check the expiration date.

- **Birth control pills:** Taken daily by women to stop ovulation (no egg = no pregnancy). When used perfectly, they're over 99% effective; if you factor in real-life mistakes, that drops to about 91%. Since the pill doesn't protect against STIs, combining it with condoms—called "dual protection"—is the smartest move.
- **Spermicide:** A chemical barrier that disables sperm. It's available as gels, foams, or films that you insert into the vagina before sex. On its own, it's only about 72% effective, but when used with condoms or diaphragms, it adds another layer of protection. Some people experience irritation from spermicide, which can actually increase STI risk if exposure happens.
- **Outercourse:** Includes anything sexual that doesn't involve penetration—like kissing, grinding, mutual masturbation, or dry humping (any sexual contact

through underwear or clothes). These activities carry no risk of pregnancy, but some STIs can still spread through skin-to-skin contact. Outercourse is a safer option, but it's not foolproof.

- **Withdrawal or pulling out:** Sounds simple, right? Pull out before you ejaculate. But pre-ejaculate (pre-cum) can contain sperm and STIs, and timing is tough to get right. That's why withdrawal is only about 78% effective at preventing pregnancy.
- If a condom breaks or there's a chance a pregnancy could result from sex, then you can get *emergency contraception* in the form of a pill from the pharmacy. Pills like Plan B must be taken by girls as soon as possible, within 72 to 120 hours, depending on the brand. The sooner, the better.
    - This is not a primary method—high hormone doses can cause side effects like nausea or irregular bleeding.

Preventing pregnancy is only part of the picture. Taking care of your sexual health means thinking beyond just birth control. Let's talk STIs.

Understanding STIs

A sexually transmitted infection is exactly what it sounds like: an infection passed between people through sexual contact. That can mean vaginal, oral, or anal sex, but some STIs spread via skin-to-skin contact or even shared fluids without penetration.

STIs generally fall into two main types:

- **Bacterial:** These include infections like *chlamydia*, *gonorrhea*, and *syphilis*. They're caused by bacteria and can usually be cured with antibiotics, if caught early. But if ignored, they can lead to serious problems. Chlamydia and gonorrhea, for example, can cause pain, damage reproductive organs, and lead to infertility. Syphilis, if left untreated long-term, can even affect your heart, brain, and nerves.
- **Viral:** These include *herpes* (*HSV*), *HPV* (*human papillomavirus*), *hepatitis* B, and *HIV*. Viral infections can't be cured, but many can be managed with medicine. For example, someone with HIV who gets proper treatment can live a long, healthy life and avoid passing it on. But without treatment, HIV weakens the immune system and becomes life-threatening. HPV can lead to cancers (including cervical, penile, or throat cancer), and herpes can cause recurring painful sores.

How Do You Know If You Have One?

You can have an STI and have zero symptoms. No pain, no rash, no weird discharge—nothing that feels off. That's why people sometimes spread STIs without realizing it. You can feel completely healthy and still pass something on to your partner.

Why Testing Matters

That's why regular testing is the responsible thing to do if you're sexually active. It's usually quick, private, and available in more places than you think—clinics, doctors' offices, and sometimes even at school or through at-home kits. In a lot of areas, you don't even need parental permission.

The tests themselves? Usually, a urine sample, a cheek swab, or a small blood draw. That's it. You'll either get results the same day or in a few days. And if something comes up, you'll get help, not judgment.

Keep It Honest

Just as important as using protection and getting tested is being straightforward with whoever you're with. Talk about your sexual history, if you've been tested, and what you're both doing to stay safe. These don't need to be intense sit-down talks with a spotlight and a mic. A simple, "Hey, just so you know, I got tested recently—how about you?" shows you're responsible and that you care.

STIs aren't something to fear—they're something to understand. With protection, testing, and honest conversations, you can stay ahead of them.

READY TO LEVEL UP?

You've just gone through the nitty-gritty of foreplay, intercourse, and protecting yourself against all the unexpected twists and turns that come with getting intimate. Sure, sex can be thrilling, sometimes awkward, but always a learning experience that's way more about connection than perfection.

So now, let's talk about that thing we called the golden rule of sex in the last chapter: consent.

Because no matter how ready you feel or how strong the chemistry is, nothing happens without a clear, enthusiastic yes—from both people, every step of the way.

Let's go there next.

SEVEN
CONSENT

Consent is what makes intimacy feel safe, mutual, and genuinely connected. When both people know what's okay—and what's not—there's more trust, less confusion, and everything works better.

Not knowing how consent works can cause real harm, even without bad intentions. So, to show up with clarity, confidence, and respect for yourself and the other person—you need to understand what consent really means and how to recognize it.

THE BASICS

Consent means an unambiguous, affirmative, and conscious decision by each person to engage in mutually agreed-upon sexual activity. Translation? It's about making sure everyone involved is 100% on board. No pressure. No confusion. Just two people choosing to connect because they both genuinely want to.

So, what does real consent look like in action?

- **Freely given:** Consent only counts if it's given without pressure or manipulation. That means no guilt trips, no begging, no wearing someone down until they give in. If someone agrees just to avoid conflict or make the other person happy, that's not real consent. A real "yes" has to come from a place of clear, informed choice —not fear, obligation, or confusion.
- **Informed:** It's like ordering food at a restaurant. You want to know what you're getting, right? You wouldn't want the waiter to bring you a spicy curry when you ordered a plain cheese pizza. With consent, it's the same deal. Everyone needs to be clear about what they're comfortable with. No surprises, no switching things up without checking in first.
- **Enthusiastic:** A real high five isn't a limp-wristed, half-hearted thing. It's all about that smack that makes your hand tingle. Consent should feel the same, confident, and clear. If someone says, "Uh, I guess," that's not a green light. That's a moment to pause, check in, and make sure you're both fully into it.
- **Ongoing:** It's like deciding you're full halfway through your meal—you don't have to force yourself to finish it if you don't want to. Just because someone agreed earlier doesn't mean they can't change their mind. If something feels off or stops being fun, it's okay to stop. Respecting that is part of showing up with emotional intelligence and trust.

Red Flags: When Consent Is Missing

Sure, a clear, confident "no" is ideal, but not everyone waves a giant red flag when they're uncomfortable about sexual contact. Sometimes, the signs are subtle, which means you need to stay alert, reading the situation like a detective piecing together clues; miss those signals and you risk crossing a line. Here's how to spot when consent has left the chat:

- **Pushy doesn't equal permission:** If someone says, "Come on, everyone's doing it," they're trying to manipulate you. Guilt trips, scare tactics, or wearing someone down until they give in? Still a "no." Don't fall for it, and don't be the one doing it.
- **Unclear means stop:** A shrug, a mumbled "I guess," or an uncomfortable laugh? That's not a green light. If someone isn't clearly into it, they're not giving consent. Sex isn't a guessing game. If you're not sure, ask. If it still feels off, don't go forward.
- **Fear shuts it down:** If someone looks tense, scared, or like they're trying to disappear into the floor, stop. A "yes" spoken through clenched teeth, or with fear in their eyes, isn't a real yes. Nobody should feel scared, pressured, or trapped in a sexual situation. Fear cancels consent.
- **Stealthing:** If someone agrees to sex with a condom, that's the deal. Taking it off without telling them—even if you think they won't notice—is called stealthing, and it's illegal. You're not just breaking trust, you're crossing a serious line. Changing the rules without their clear okay is assault. Don't go there.
- **Freezing means no:** Sometimes, people don't say "no" because they freeze. If someone suddenly goes quiet, goes still, or zones out, don't ignore it. That silence isn't approval—it could mean fear, shock, or panic.

Check in, stop what you're doing, and make sure they're safe and okay.

- **Actions speak louder:** If they're pulling away, flinching, turning their head, or trying to leave, that's a non-verbal *no.* You have to pay attention. If their body says they're uncomfortable, you stop. No second-guessing, no pushing through.

The key rule to remember? If it's not a confident, enthusiastic "yes," it's a no. And when in doubt, just ask.

REAL CONNECTION STARTS WITH REAL CLARITY

When both people are genuinely into it, everything clicks better. The vibe, the connection, the trust—it all starts with one simple thing: consent and being crystal clear. No guessing games. No wishful thinking. No, just assuming things are cool.

And yeah, it takes some guts to slow things down and actually check in. But that's also what being mature is all about. Anyone can just go with the flow. It takes more to actually respect the moment and the person right there with you.

But what happens when things aren't so clear-cut? When someone's had a few drinks? When do the signals feel crossed? When you're not sure if they're actually feeling it or just trying to play it cool?

That's what we're diving into next because real respect shows up, not just when it's easy, but when it really matters.

EIGHT
THE ROLE OF SUBSTANCES IN CONSENT

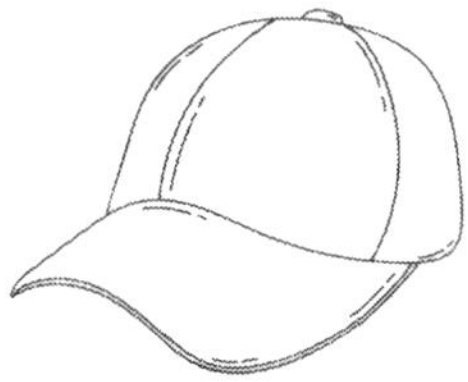

We've talked about how important clarity is when it comes to consent. But what happens when alcohol or drugs enter the picture? That clarity takes a nosedive. Suddenly, it's like trying to read a book with all the pages scrambled—not exactly ideal for making important decisions.

HOW SUBSTANCES HIJACK CONSENT

Substances have a sneaky way of hijacking your brain's control center. Here's some quick science: alcohol and drugs mess with your prefrontal cortex—the part of your brain responsible for judgment, self-control, and decision-making. It's like your brain's "responsible adult," and when substances are involved, that adult takes a nap. What's left running the show? Your impulsive, emotional side that doesn't always think, "What could go wrong?"

Let's break down exactly what happens:

- **Judgment goes out the window:** The part of the brain that says, "This is a bad idea," gets muted. What's left is a risky mix of overconfidence and poor decision-making.
- **Mixed signals everywhere:** Substances blur body language and tone, making it hard to tell if someone's laughing because they're having fun or because they feel awkward and uncomfortable.
- **The morning after disconnect:** Once the fog lifts, reality snaps back. That decision you celebrated last night can feel confusing. What felt like a consensual moment can turn into regret, shame, or trauma because your brain wasn't fully online to give or receive clear consent.

Now, picture someone in that state trying to give consent. Even if they seem into it, their brain isn't firing on all cylinders, which means meaningful consent just isn't possible.

REAL-LIFE SCENARIOS WHERE CONSENT GOES OFF THE RAILS

It's clear that substances and consent don't mix, but what does all of this look like in real-life situations?

The Party Invite

You're at a house party. Music's blasting, people are laughing, and someone passes you a drink. Your friend Sam, who's had a few already, is joking around and getting extra chatty. Later, Sam leans in and says, "Wanna head outside?" Sam's stumbling a little, but you figure, hey, they're just tipsy.

Here's the truth: Sam's slurred words and shaky movements aren't just signs that they've had a "fun" night. They are signs that they're not in a place to make decisions, especially about anything physical. Even if Sam seems flirty, the responsible move is to steer the conversation somewhere safe (maybe toward water and fresh air) and let them sober up.

The Late-Night Dare

It's a small group hangout, and someone suggests playing Truth or Dare. Things start innocently—"Call your crush!" or "Wear socks on your hands for 10 minutes." But as the night goes on, people get bolder. Someone dares your friend Alex to kiss you. Alex has had a drink, and while they laugh nervously, they eventually shrug and lean in.

This is where the brakes hit. Alex's hesitation is a clear signal that they're not fully into it, and the alcohol adds another layer of uncertainty. Even if it's "just a game," forcing a moment like this can leave someone feeling awkward or regretful the next day.

HANDLING CONSENT IN SUBSTANCE-FUELED MOMENTS

The real flex is knowing when to pause. If substances are involved and something feels off—even a little—don't guess your way through it.

Respecting boundaries in these situations not only helps you avoid trouble, but it also helps you build trust and shows that you value the other person as much as they deserve to be valued.

So if anything feels unclear, here's your move:

1. **Check their state:** Are they making eye contact? Speaking clearly? Standing without swaying like a tree

in a hurricane? If the answer is "no," intimacy is off the table.

2. **Ask directly:** A simple, "Are you feeling okay?" or "Do you really want to do this?" can reveal a lot. If they hesitate, stop.
3. **Prioritize sobriety:** When in doubt, save physical closeness for a time when both of you are sober and clear-headed. You'll thank yourself for it.

Being a decent human means respecting someone's boundaries, especially when they're not in a state to fully articulate them. Alcohol and drugs are no excuse to blur the lines or ignore cues. Because when you ignore those cues, it can become something more serious.

Next, we'll explore what crossing the line means, how to recognize it, and what to do if it happens to you or someone else.

NINE
SEXUAL VIOLENCE

Sexual violence isn't a "grown-ups only" problem. It happens in crowded hallways between classes, in a friend's basement after the lights go low, and in late-night DMs. Chances are you already know someone—a classmate, a teammate, or maybe even yourself—who has been closer to it than anyone should be.

This is the hard truth:

- In the U.S., about 1 in 9 girls and 1 in 20 boys experience sexual abuse or assault before they turn 18. Since most guys don't report it, that second number is probably higher.
- In England and Wales, police recorded almost 200,000 reports of sexual offences in 2024 and over a third of those were rapes.
- In both places, 9 out of 10 times, the people causing harm are guys. Not monsters from crime shows, but ordinary guys who either never learned the rules or decided they didn't apply to them.

These numbers aren't here to scare you. They're a reality check.

We'll break sexual violence into four clear categories so you can understand exactly where the legal lines are—and how to make sure you don't cross them.

Read on and lock it in.

COERCION

Coercion is a pressure tactic. It's when someone gets pushed into doing something sexual through guilt, manipulation, subtle threats, or just not letting up until they give in. It's when "no" gets ignored long enough that it turns into a tired "fine."

What It Looks Like

Let's say you're with someone you're dating. You want things to get physical, but they're not into it. Maybe they say, "I'm not comfortable with that right now," or "Let's just chill." Instead of listening, you keep pushing. You ask again. You act hurt. You might even hint that if they don't do it, someone else will.

Eventually, they give a small nod or stop arguing—not because they want to, but because they want the pressure to stop. That's coercion.

It can also look like:

- repeatedly asking after someone has already said no
- using guilt, like "If you really cared about me, you would"
- making them feel bad for having boundaries
- acting like they owe you something
- making them worry you'll break up with them if they say no

What the Law Says

Laws vary depending on where you live, but in both the US and the UK, if someone agrees to sex only because they feel pushed or cornered, that's not considered valid consent. Even if "sexual coercion" isn't always listed as a separate crime, any sexual contact that happens after someone's been pressured can still be charged as assault or rape.

If someone doesn't feel safe or free to say no, they're not really able to say yes. If you push until they give in, you've crossed the line.

SEXUAL ASSAULT

Sexual assault is any sexual activity—everything from unwanted touching or kissing to more severe acts—that happens without clear and willing agreement. Pay attention to that word: agreement.

What It Looks Like

You're hanging out with someone you like. You're watching something, sitting close. You make a move—put your hand on their thigh or try to kiss them. They go quiet, lean away a little, or shift their body. Maybe they say nothing at all. You keep going because they didn't stop you.

That's not okay. Just because someone doesn't push you off doesn't mean they're into it. No one should have to fight you off to be respected.

Sexual assault can look like:

- sliding your hand under your clothes without checking in
- hugging or dancing in a way that pins someone in place

- pressing against someone in a crowd or hallway
- snapping a bra strap or slapping someone's butt
- using a "game" or teasing to excuse unwanted touching

Also:

- **It doesn't have to be violent:** If someone didn't want it and you did it anyway, it's serious—even without yelling or fighting.
- **Being drunk doesn't excuse you:** If you're drunk, you're still fully responsible for what you do.
- **Watch body language:** If they're tense, quiet, or trying to get space, that's your cue to stop.

What the Law Says

The legal definition of sexual assault is pretty consistent around the world: it's any kind of sexual contact that happens without consent. The consequences depend on where you live and what happened. But even the lowest-level charges are serious, we're talking:

- **Misdemeanor:** Charges can mean fines, mandatory counseling, and a criminal record.
- **Felony:** Charges can lead to years in prison, thousands in fines, and permanent registration as a sex offender.
- **Sex offender registration:** Means your name, photo, and conviction go into a public database—often for life.

If there's doubt, don't do it. There's no excuse strong enough to justify ignoring someone's boundaries.

RAPE

This is the most serious line you can cross. Rape is defined as any kind of penetration—vaginal, anal, or oral—without full, clear, and ongoing consent. This includes using a body part or an object. There's no gray area.

What It Looks Like

You're in a bedroom with someone. Things are heating up, and they're into it at first. But then something shifts. They stiffen, pull back a little, or say something like "I don't want to go further." You pause—but only for a second. Maybe you assume they're just nervous, or you think they'll change their mind. So you keep going. That moment right there? That's when the line gets crossed.

This includes:

- **Coercion.**
- **Stealthing**.

Why Does This Matter?

Rape causes deep emotional, psychological and physical wounds. Survivors often carry it for years or their whole lives. It can lead to trauma, anxiety, panic attacks, depression, trust issues, and fear that show up in ways most people never see. It can take away someone's sense of safety in their own body.

What the Law Says

If you're the person who crosses that line, the consequences are just as real. In the U.S., rape is a felony in every single state. That can mean decades in prison, heavy fines, and being added to a public sex offender registry for the rest of your life. That label doesn't just follow you—it defines where you can live, who will hire you, and how others see you. In the UK, rape carries a maximum sentence of life in prison.

Moral of the story? If there's even a flicker of hesitation, stop. Not later, right then. There's no moment, no hookup, no fantasy worth risking someone's safety or your freedom.

STATUTORY RAPE

Statutory rape means having sex with someone who is below the legal age of consent, no matter the circumstances. It doesn't matter if they said yes. It doesn't matter if they were the ones who made the first move. It doesn't even matter if they lied about how old they were. If they're under the legal age, the law says they cannot give valid consent, and you are the one held responsible.

What It Looks Like

You're 16. You meet someone through friends, you hit it off, you flirt, and eventually you hook up. They told you they were 16, but later, you find out they're actually 14. Even though they said yes and everything felt mutual, it doesn't matter. The law states that a 14-year-old cannot legally consent to sex. That makes what happened statutory rape.

What You Need to Remember

- **Age of consent varies:** Usually between 16–18

- **The older person is responsible:** For knowing the law
- **Statutory rape = felony:** That can mean prison, fines, and lifelong sex offender status.

If you're not 100% sure of someone's age—or if they're under the age of consent where you are—don't go there. Their "yes" won't protect you in court, and the consequences can follow you for life.

WHAT TO DO IF YOU'VE BEEN HARMED

Now, this needs to be made crystal clear: sexual abuse doesn't just happen to girls. Boys and young men can be victims, too. It can come from women, men, older teens, or even family members.

If something happened that felt wrong, confusing, forced, or left you with a sick feeling in your stomach, it matters. Your experience is real. Being harmed doesn't make you "weak," and it doesn't take anything away from your masculinity. It means someone crossed a line they never should have.

Here are your options:

- **Talk to someone you trust:** This is often the hardest step, but it's also the most powerful. A parent, a coach, a teacher, a counselor, an older sibling, a friend's parent—any adult who listens without judgment. Just saying it out loud can start to take the weight off.
- **Reach out to support services:** There are trained people whose entire job is to help survivors of sexual violence.
    - In the **U.S.**, contact the National Sexual Assault Hotline at 800-656-HOPE or visit RAINN.org.

    - In the **U.K.**, check out Rape Crisis England & Wales or SurvivorsUK (specifically for male survivors). These services are free, private, and judgment-free.
- **It's not your fault:** No matter how you acted, what you drank, or whether you froze up instead of fighting back. You are never responsible for someone else's decision to hurt you.
- **You're not weak for needing help:** Asking for support after trauma is one of the strongest, most grown-up things you can do. It shows you value yourself enough to heal.
- **You're not alone:** Millions of people—yes, including guys—have gone through this and come out the other side. You can heal, too. It takes time, but it's possible.

You deserve to feel safe in your own body. You deserve to be heard, believed, and supported. No matter what anyone told you—or what you've told yourself—it's never too late to speak up or start healing.

WHAT TO DO IF YOU HARMED SOMEONE

This part is tough, but it's critical. If reading this chapter stirred something in you, if you're sitting with that sinking feeling in your chest, wondering if maybe you crossed a line, pressured someone, touched them without full consent, or hurt them in ways you didn't understand at the time, don't brush that feeling off.

Feeling ashamed, afraid, angry, or deeply confused right now is human. But those feelings don't erase what happened. What matters now is what you do with that discomfort.

Here's what you can do:

- **Stop the behavior immediately:** If you're still engaging in anything manipulative, pressuring, or non-consensual—whether it's touching, texting, sending photos, or pushing boundaries in any way—you need to stop. Right now. Full stop. This isn't negotiable.
- **Figure out exactly what went wrong:** Don't just sit with guilt—get informed. Reread this chapter. Look up credible resources on consent, coercion, and abuse. Learn how power, pressure, and silence affect people's ability to say no. The goal is to fully understand the harm, so you never repeat it.
- **Talk to someone qualified:** Find a counselor, therapist, or adult trained in this area—someone who can help you face what you've done with honesty and compassion, without letting you off the hook. This isn't about fixing your image. It's about doing the real, long-term work of repair and accountability. And yes—if your actions were criminal, you may need legal advice too. That's part of the responsibility.
- **Consider an apology:** Wanting to make it right is good, but apologies are complicated. An apology should never be about easing your guilt or trying to "fix things." It should center on the person you harmed. Sometimes, the best apology isn't words—it's making sure they never have to deal with your harm again. In some cases, reaching out might reopen wounds or feel manipulative. A therapist or counselor can help you decide if, when, and how an apology could be safe and appropriate.

Owning your past actions won't erase the past, but it's the only path to genuine change and building true integrity.

RESPONSIBILITY, CULTURE, AND CHANGE

Sexual violence doesn't just materialize out of nowhere. It starts with a culture that treats pressure as flirting, silence as permission, and disrespect as no big deal.

You can help change that. Here's how:

- **Call out your friends:** If someone says something creepy or crosses a line, don't brush it off. Even a simple "Dude, not cool" can shift the vibe. You don't need to make a speech—just show that you're not okay with it.
- **Don't stay silent:** If someone looks uncomfortable, is being pressured, or seems out of it, step in. Ask if they're okay. Change the subject. Get a trusted adult. Being the one who interrupts might feel awkward, but it could save someone from serious harm.
- **Check your group chat:** What gets posted, joked about, or passed around in private says a lot about what you think is okay. If the memes are degrading or the comments would make someone feel unsafe in real life, it's time to rethink what you're laughing at.
- **Practice respect daily:** It's not about being a hero in some big moment. It's about the everyday stuff: how you talk about people, how you handle rejection, and how you treat boundaries. Respect isn't a switch you flip —it's a habit you build.
- **Shape the culture:** Every time you speak up, every time you choose not to laugh, and every time you respect someone's "no" without argument—you're setting a standard. You're making it harder for the next line to be crossed.

The lines are not blurry. Not anymore. You know now, and that makes you responsible for what you do and what you allow around you.

You don't have to have all the answers. You just have to care enough to act with integrity and be brave enough to hold others to that same standard.

Now let's see what you've picked up! You've read, thought, and maybe even felt a little uncomfortable (that's okay too). Let's lock it in with the quiz.

QUIZ: SEX, CONSENT, AND RESPECT

Pick the answer that feels right for each question, then see how you did in the answer key at the back of the book.

1. **Which method is the only single option that helps prevent both pregnancy *and* most STIs?**
    a. Birth-control pills
    b. Condoms
    c. Withdrawal (pull-out)
2. **Why does regular STI testing matter even when you feel totally healthy?**
    a. Many STIs show zero symptoms, so testing is the only way to know
    b. Clinics need to use their test kits before they expire
    c. Testing replaces the need for protection
3. **Which scenario makes consent *invalid*?**
    a. A clear, enthusiastic yes from both people
    b. A yes given while confused, pressured, or scared
    c. A mutual plan set and agreed upon in advance
4. **What defines statutory rape?**
    a. Sex that involves physical force
    b. Sex with someone below the legal age of consent—even if they say yes
    c. Consensual sex between two teens the same age
5. **Which dating behavior is a red flag for a toxic relationship?**
    a. Respecting your need for space with friends
    b. Demanding your phone password and constant updates
    c. Listening to your opinions during disagreements

6. **What does *enthusiastic consent* sound or look like?**
   a. A shrug followed by "I guess"
   b. An excited, pressure-free yes that can change at any time
   c. Silence interpreted as approval
7. **Aftercare—checking in once sex is over—can include:**
   a. Ignoring each other and scrolling social media
   b. Cuddling or talking to be sure both people feel comfortable
   c. Posting details online for friends
8. **Which activity carries no pregnancy risk but can *still* pass some STIs?**
   a. Outercourse (kissing, grinding, mutual masturbation)
   b. Vaginal sex with a condom
   c. Withdrawal during intercourse

PART THREE
THE ONLINE WORLD AND ME

TEN

THE INTERNET AND YOU

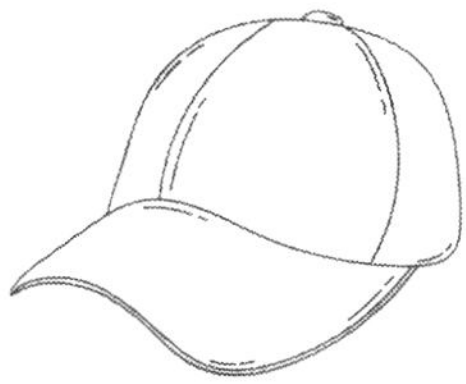

The internet is everywhere—on your phone, your laptop, your gaming console, even your watch. It gives you access to anything you could want to know, see, or experience—and plenty you probably don't.

The problem? There's no manual. No one really teaches you how to deal with the constant stream of information, images, and opinions hitting you every day. Some of it's helpful. Some of it's just for fun. And some of it can seriously mess with your head if you're not ready for it.

To use it well, you need to understand how it works. These are a few smart moves and a bit of information to help you stay in control, no matter how loud your notifications get.

THE SYSTEM IS WORKING

You pick up your phone for one notification, a few taps later, you're watching a raccoon flip pancakes while strangers argue about sandwich rankings in the comments. You didn't plan to open that app. You didn't plan to scroll. But now it's 20 minutes later, and you still haven't replied to your mom.

It's not that you're "easily distracted," these apps are designed to pull you in fast and keep you there as long as possible.

Step One: Get Your Attention

Social media isn't free because the people who made it are generous. It's free because your attention is what's being sold.

Every time you scroll, pause on a video, like a post, or click a link, the app learns something about you. Then it uses that information to give you more of what keeps you locked in. If it's movie clips, you'll get more movie clips. If it's memes, gaming rants, conspiracy theories, or chaotic slime videos, you'll keep seeing those too.

The longer you stay, the more ads you see. The more ads you see, the more money they make. It's that simple. Your attention is their business model, and business is booming.

Step Two: Mess With Your Head

As the algorithm gets better at holding your attention, the content you see starts to influence how you think, how you feel about yourself, and how you see the world. But how does that actually happen?

When you scroll, your brain gets flooded with images of people looking amazing, achieving big things, or living lives that seem effortlessly perfect. Whether it's posed, filtered, or staged doesn't matter. Your brain often reacts as if it's real.

That's because seeing "better-than-life" content triggers a comparison loop in your brain, especially in areas tied to self-evaluation and reward. Studies show that the more time teens spend on social media, the more likely they are to compare themselves to others, and the more comparison, the higher the risk of anxiety, depression, and low self-esteem.

Suddenly, the voice in your head shifts: Should I look like that? Should I have that setup? Why does their life seem so much cooler than mine?

Even small things—a group photo you're not in, a couple's cute moment, someone's post about their latest win—can hit harder than you expect. Without meaning to, your brain starts doing exactly what it was wired to do: scan, compare, and judge. Social media just exploits that wiring, over and over again.

Step Three: Train You to Perform

Pretty soon, it's not just about what you're *seeing*. It's about what you're *doing*.

You start thinking about what you post. You pause before you share something, wondering if it's going to get enough likes or if someone's going to say something dumb in the comments.

Maybe you try to come off chill, funny, smooth—whatever version of yourself feels like it'll get the least pushback. Not because you're fake, but because you've been trained to think about how stuff plays instead of how it feels.

You start living with a kind of filter in your head, constantly asking: Should I take a pic of this? Would this make a good post? Is this moment even worth anything if nobody sees it?

Even if you're barely posting at all, that pressure can still be there. Just knowing you could post makes you see yourself from the outside. Like you're being watched, even when you're alone.

Step Four: Let It Run the Show

Eventually, this stuff stops feeling like a choice and starts feeling automatic. You check your phone without even realizing it, and over time, all that casual checking in starts to add up. Not just in screen time, but in how you feel, how you sleep, how your brain works.

Here's what it does behind the scenes:

- **Brain fog:** Jumping between apps, videos, messages, and notifications keeps your brain in constant "switch mode." You can't focus deeply on anything because your attention is scattered in five directions at once. Homework feels harder, reading takes longer, and you're mentally wiped without even knowing why.
- **Sleep wreckage:** Late-night scrolling messes with your sleep cycle. The blue light blocks melatonin (the sleep hormone), so you stay up later, fall asleep slower, and wake up groggier—even after hours in bed.
- **Low-key stress:** Notifications. Group chats. Social pressure. The "need" to keep up, respond fast, look good, know what's going on—it all builds this constant, low-level anxiety. You feel on edge, even when nothing's technically wrong.
- **Physical burnout:** Your body takes a hit too. Sore thumbs, tight shoulders, stiff neck from always looking down. Even headaches from screen glare. Your muscles are basically saying, *Bro. Enough.*
- **Disconnection from real life:** You might be surrounded by people you like, but still feel kind of... distant. Half-there. Like your brain's buffering. That sense of being zoned out or "off" is your system running low on actual rest and real interactions.

TAKING BACK THE REINS

You don't have to quit your phone, swear off social media, or go live in a cabin with no Wi-Fi. But if you want to feel more in control of your brain, your time, and your energy, you do need to start using your phone *on your terms*, not the algorithm's.

Here's how to start pulling some control back:

- **Silence the noise:** Turn off non-essential notifications. You don't need a buzz for every like, retweet, or random app update. Keep the stuff that actually matters—calls, close contacts, emergencies. Mute the rest. Peace is underrated.
- **Create no-phone zones:** Pick times or places where your phone just doesn't get to come. During meals. During homework. The hour before bed. When you're hanging out with people in real life. Give your brain a chance to be fully present.
- **Switch it up:** If your phone has become your everything—alarm clock, notebook, entertainment, camera, escape hatch—it might help to divide the load. Read a real book. Jot things down on paper. Use a laptop for research. Even small shifts can help.
- **Do something that actually fuels you:** Real life hits different. Get outside, build something, play music, work out, paint, hang out with your friends in person. Whatever reconnects you to *you*, do more of that.

You've seen how the scroll can creep in, shape how you think, and slowly take the wheel. Noticing that is step one. Choosing to shift things is how you start driving again.

Now there's one more part of digital life that deserves a little more clarity.

ELEVEN
WHAT PORN PROMISES

Let's talk about porn. Around 73% of teens aged 13 to 17 have seen porn, and more than half were under 13 the first time they did.

That first experience usually doesn't come with a warning label or a conversation. It's just there—one click away. And when no one explains what you're seeing, it's easy to assume porn is a normal part of sex, or worse, that it's what sex *should* look like. But is that actually true?

THE REALITY BEHIND THE FANTASY

Porn sells a very specific kind of story: perfect bodies, dramatic scenes, zero conversation, and everything going smoothly from the first second. Well, it looks slick for a reason:

- **Actors:** Picked based on what the industry thinks will "sell."
- **Scenes are scripted and reshot:** Multiple takes. Flattering lighting. Careful editing. Anything that

doesn't feed the fantasy—hesitation, changing your mind, asking a question—gets cut.

- **The connection is performative:** No genuine emotional bond. No aftercare. No "Are you okay?" Just action, zoomed in, intensified, and looped.

What you're watching is a manufactured performance, not a real moment between real people. The more you see it, the more it can start to shift your expectations about sex, about bodies, about what it's supposed to "look" and "feel" like.

So let's look at what it actually does to your brain.

WHY IT MATTERS TO YOU

1. **Body image issues:** Watching too much porn can make you hyper-aware of how you look, from your muscles to your hairline. When what you see on screen feels unattainable, it's easy to feel like you're falling short.
2. **Relationship problems:** If you start to think intimacy should look like what you've seen in porn, real-life connections can feel awkward or underwhelming. Those moments of trust and laughter—what actually makes relationships great—don't show up on camera.
3. **Addiction and escalation:** The dopamine boost you get from watching porn can turn into a habit. Over time, you might find yourself needing more extreme content to feel the same level of interest, which can mess with your views on healthy boundaries.

Porn is one part of digital life that's easy to fall into, but harder to think clearly about. It's personal, it's private, and it's often treated like a joke or a secret, which means no one really helps you make sense of it.

So here's the reminder: porn is not a how-to guide. It's not where you should be learning about connection, or sex, or what you're "supposed" to look or act like. Curiosity is normal. But you deserve better information than an edited performance.

Talk to people you trust. Read things that don't sell you a fantasy. Learn what real connection actually feels like—for you. Because you get to shape that, and it doesn't have to look anything like a screen.

THE BIGGER PICTURE

You now get how these digital systems are built—designed to hook you, subtly steer your actions, and even mess with your idea of normal. This knowledge puts the power back in your hands to decide what you give your time, energy, and mind to.

And after zooming out on the internet and porn, it's a good time to zoom back in—to the daily stuff. The group chats, the late-night DMs, the way we treat each other when we're behind a screen. That's where we're headed next.

Up next: Digital Manners.

TWELVE

DIGITAL MANNERS

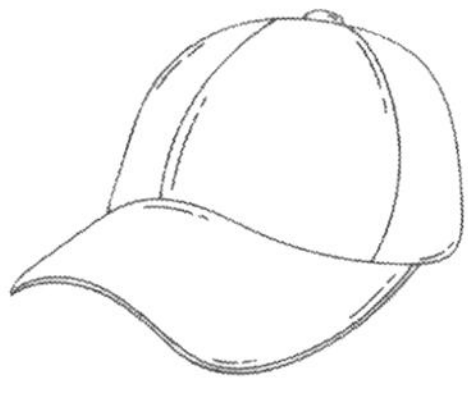

In a world where relationships can start with something as simple as a double-tap or a clever meme, it makes sense that consent matters in digital spaces. Even when the internet feels like the Wild West, the same rules still apply: be clear, be respectful, and make sure everyone involved agrees.

WHY DOES DIGITAL CONSENT MATTER?

You wouldn't walk into someone's room without knocking first, right? In the online world, asking for permission works the same way. The only difference is you're knocking with words.

Screens can make everything feel casual, low-stakes, no big deal. But the truth is, what you say or post or share still impacts real people. Even if you meant it as a joke. Even if you didn't think it would matter.

When those digital boundaries get ignored, people can get hurt. A 2022 study found that around 59% of teens had been harassed or bullied online. Sure, some of that came from strangers—but a surprising amount came from people they actually knew. Friends. Classmates. Exes.

And what comes after that? Often, regret. Almost 1 in 3 teens said they'd posted something they later wished they hadn't. Usually, it involved someone else.

So what does doing it right even look like?

How to be a Good Digital Citizen

It starts with remembering that behind every username is a real person. A person with their own limits, their own feelings, and their own idea of what's funny—and what's just... not.

Brushing it off with "Relax, it's just a meme" or "It was only a story" doesn't make it okay. If someone's uncomfortable, then it matters.

Being respectful online means thinking about:

- Who's part of the moment you're sharing
- What kind of content is it?
- How might it feel to the person on the other side?

Not sure if it's fine to post? Tissue to connect with the breakdown.

Post, Tag, Share... Then Ask?

Let's zoom in on something that happens all the time: sharing a funny moment.

Imagine you catch your friend doing the world's most epic face-plant. It's hilarious—maybe they tripped on an invisible banana peel, or they're reenacting a dance move gone wrong. You can already imagine the likes rolling in if you post the video.

But hold up: even if it's comedic gold to you, your friend might not find it so funny. A quick "Yo, is it cool if I share this?" can prevent a meltdown, preserve the friendship, and save them from being the butt of jokes they never asked for.

This doesn't just apply to your main feed, either. Group chats can be a digital war zone in disguise. Screenshots bounce around faster than you can say "Wait, don't share that!" A private joke in a tiny chat can turn into a campus-wide rumor in minutes if it falls into the wrong hands.

Before you type something—especially if it's sensitive or personal—ask yourself: "Would I say this to their face? Would I be okay if this got out?" If the answer is nope, maybe keep it out of the chat.

The Screenshot Snag

You know how this goes. Apps like Snapchat advertise disappearing messages, but screenshots can keep them alive forever, or someone with a second phone can record your snap in seconds.

Even if someone means well, saying "I gotta show someone this" can spiral fast. What started as a private moment becomes a group chat joke, then maybe a full-blown rumor.

Sure, privacy settings help, but they're not foolproof. Friends forward stuff. "Private" posts get screenshotted. Curiosity spreads fast, and control slips away the moment you hit send.

So here's the move: treat every snap, DM, or post like it *could* be shared. If you wouldn't be okay with that, don't send it.

When Tech Turns Creepy

Respecting digital consent doesn't stop at what you post. It also includes how you treat someone's privacy.

Maybe you've seen couples or friends sharing passcodes or tracking apps. That's not always a red flag—if both people are totally on board. But when it becomes one-sided, or someone feels like they have to say yes just to avoid a fight? That's control, not trust.

A 2021 survey found that about 26% of teens had felt pressured by a partner to hand over passwords or access to their accounts.

Real trust doesn't need 24/7 access. If someone's demanding your passwords, reading your DMs, or using an app to follow your every move, that's a red flag. If it's happening to you—or if you've been the one crossing that line—it's time to stop.

Everyone deserves digital privacy, no matter how close the relationship is.

When You Do It Right

When you are a good digital citizen:

- People trust you.
- There's less drama.
- You don't wake up to angry texts or guilt-tripping messages about something you posted.
- Plus, being the one who doesn't screenshot, blast a private convo, or post without asking gives you a solid reputation.

In other words, everyone wins.

Now, not all online interactions are as innocent as tagging your mate in a "fail" video. Sometimes, things move beyond memes and jokes into personal, intimate territory.

SEXTING: WHY THAT "ONE LITTLE PHOTO" ISN'T SO LITTLE

Sexting means sending—or being asked to send—intimate photos, videos, or texts. On-screen, it feels like just one tap. Off-screen, it carries more weight.

Odds are you're more likely to ask than be asked. Maybe things are getting flirty with someone you like. The vibe's good. The messages are picking up. Then you're tempted to say it: "Send me a pic?" It might feel like something guys do. Or maybe you're thinking, "Wait, is this normal?"

It might seem like no big deal because "everyone's doing it." But is everyone? And even if they are, does that automatically make it a good idea?

Why Do People Sext Anyway?

Sexting is common enough that some people see it as just another step in flirting. One study found that about 27% of teens aged 12–17 have received nudes, and around 15% have sent them (Haelle, 2018). Sometimes it's curiosity. Sometimes it feels like closeness. Sometimes it's pure peer pressure.

For guys, that pressure often starts with friends. Nudes get talked about like trophies—something to show off, collect, or stash for clout. In the moment, it might sound cool, but it treats the person on the other end like an object, not a human.

The double standard is real, too. Plenty of girls get slammed either way—"easy" if they send, "boring" if they don't. Nobody wins in that setup.

And beyond the social mess, in a lot of places is illegal to create or share explicit images of anyone under 18—even if both people are teens. That "just between us" photo can turn into a legal nightmare.

How to Handle the Moment

Whether you're thinking of sending something or wanting to ask, here's how to avoid getting caught in a mess:

If you're thinking about sending:

- **Pause and reflect:** Are you doing this because you want to or because you feel like you have to?
- **Think beyond now:** Can you trust this person with something that could live forever? Spoiler: if you're unsure, the answer is no.

If you're thinking about asking:

- **Check your motives:** Are you asking because you care about them, or because you think it's "what everyone does"?
- **Respect their response:** If they hesitate or say no, drop it. Pushing further isn't cute—it's coercion.

Here's a better move: skip the risky request and build trust instead through conversation or shared interests. Real connection beats a risky pic every time.

How to Bounce Back If You Messed Up

Stuff happens. Maybe you sent a pic and now regret it. Or you asked, and it didn't go over well. What matters is how you handle it:

- **If you sent something:**
  - **Ask for deletion:** A simple, "Hey, I'm not comfortable with that being out there—please delete it" can go a long way.
  - **Talk to someone you trust:** Whether it's a parent, teacher, or counselor, looping in an adult can help if things escalate.
- **If you pressured someone:**
  - **Own up:** Apologize for crossing a line. Something like, "I'm sorry I made you uncomfortable—that wasn't okay," can help rebuild trust.

The Real Power Move? Saying No

Sexting isn't a requirement for flirting or relationships. Saying no isn't boring—it's bold.

- **For the sender:** Saying no protects your privacy, your reputation, and your peace of mind.
- **For the requester:** Respecting boundaries shows maturity and builds real trust, which is way cooler than a risky photo.

Sexting is not only about a photo—it's about trust, respect, and knowing your worth. If someone can't value you without a picture, they're not worth your time.

RESPECT STARTS WITH YOU

Understanding digital consent isn't just about doing right by others—it's also about recognizing your own limits, your own values, and your own power. The more clearly you get what respect looks like—

online or off—the easier it is to notice when something starts messing with that.

Now, let's lock in what you've learned so far with the quick quiz up next—no stress, just a chance to see which boundaries and online habits you already own and which ones could use a tune-up.

QUIZ: SCROLL SMART

Choose the answer that feels right for each question. Keep it honest, then flip to the answer key at the back of the book to see how you scored.

1. **Why do major social media apps work so hard to keep you scrolling?**
   a. To teach you important life skills
   b. To make money by selling your attention to advertisers
   c. To boost global literacy rates
2. **How can endless highlight-reel posts hurt your self-esteem over time?**
   a. They always show accurate information about real life
   b. You compare yourself to filtered, "perfect" images and feel you don't measure up
   c. They expose you to new hobbies you might enjoy
3. **What's a core rule of digital consent before sharing someone else's photo or message?**
   a. Share first—apologize later if they're upset
   b. Always ask the person's permission before you hit post, forward, or screenshot
   c. Consent isn't needed online if the content is funny
4. **Why can the screenshot feature turn a "disappearing" snap into a long-term problem?**
   a. Screenshots instantly delete themselves after 24 hours
   b. A screenshot—or even a second phone—can preserve the image forever

   c. Snapchat blocks all screenshots automatically

5. **Why is porn a terrible how-to guide for real-life intimacy?**
   a. It's filmed in one take with no editing
   b. Scenes are scripted performances that skip genuine consent, conversation, and aftercare
   c. It accurately represents most teens' experiences
6. **If a partner demands your phone passcode or tracks your location 24/7, that's a sign of:**
   a. Healthy transparency
   b. Controlling behavior and a major red flag
   c. Standard relationship etiquette
7. **Which habit helps you take back control from the algorithm?**
   a. Turning off non-essential notifications and creating no-phone zones
   b. Posting more often so the app "gets to know you"
   c. Using every social platform at the same time
8. **If someone shares a private photo of you without permission, it's:**
   a. Harmless online fun
   b. A serious violation of your privacy and digital consent
   c. Free publicity, you should appreciate

PART FOUR
THE DANGER ZONE

THIRTEEN
THE SNEAKY GRIP OF ADDICTION

Addiction isn't just a bad habit that you can shake off like a cringey nickname. It's a pattern that hijacks your brain's reward system—making things like gaming, porn, or social media feel as necessary as food or water.

The tricky part? Once those patterns lock in, they're tough to break. It's like having your favorite song stuck on repeat—only it starts drowning out everything else.

This isn't about willpower or weakness. It's about knowing how these patterns work so you can spot them early—*before* they start running the show.

HOW ADDICTION TAKES HOLD

Your brain is a total reward fan. It's like your personal hype man, throwing out dopamine—that feel-good brain juice—whenever something even remotely cool happens. Crush a good meal? Dopamine. Beat a tough game level? Dopamine. Get a text from someone you're into? You guessed it—dopamine.

This reward system is meant to help you learn what feels good and keep you motivated. But certain substances (like nicotine, alcohol, or drugs) and habits (like gambling or nonstop screen time) take advantage of it. They don't just nudge the reward button—they slam it, and you get hit with an unnatural dopamine tsunami.

That first time? Yeah, it might feel intense. The rush, the buzz, the sudden shift in mood—it can seem like a quick fix when you're stressed, bored, or just looking to feel something. But your brain catches on quick. Even if something feels amazing at first, it won't hit the same way for long. The more you do it, the less it works. What used to be enough doesn't cut it anymore?

So to chase that same high, you start to crank things up: more time, more risk, more of everything. That's called tolerance, and it's how addiction slips in through the side door. You don't even see it coming until you're stuck in the loop:

1. You take a hit (or game, or gamble, or drink) → The brain throws you a dopamine party.
2. The dopamine wears off → You crash, feeling worse than square one.
3. Cravings go nuclear → You dive back in, chasing that "good" feeling.
4. Brain's like, "Whatever, more dopamine needed!" → Tolerance cranks up again.

And before you're all, "Psh, addiction? I'm good," listen: some brains are wired to cling harder than others.

If you've got ADHD, anxiety, depression, autism, or a history of trauma, that reward system may lock on even faster. Your brain can mistake that artificial high for actual safety or comfort, which makes the pull even stronger.

One "no big deal" moment can quietly turn into a habit, and

knowing how that happens is what helps you spot the risks hiding in things like nicotine, alcohol, or weed before they take over.

ALCOHOL: THE TRUTH BEHIND THE BOTTLE

Let's start with a classic: alcohol. Maybe you've seen it at family gatherings, in TV shows, or basically every music video where someone's living it up. So it's easy to think, "If it's legal for adults, how bad can it be for me?"

Well, let's slow that roll a sec.

What *Is* Alcohol?

Alcohol is a chemical. The kind people drink is called ethanol, and it shows up in beer, wine, and liquor (also known as "spirits"). Each type packs a different punch:

- **Beer:** 4–6% alcohol
- **Wine:** 9–14%
- **Spirits (vodka, rum, whiskey):** usually 40% or more

So when someone's doing shots, they're not "just having a drink" —they're throwing back a concentrated dose that hits fast and hits hard.

What Does Alcohol Do to Your Brain and Body?

Your brain is still leveling up until you're around 25. It's still building the connections that make you faster, smarter, and better at everything. Now imagine messing with that process every weekend. It's like spilling soda on your controller right in the middle of an important boss fight.

The Science

Alcohol doesn't just "get you drunk." What it really does is mess with the way your brain works in real time. All those things you feel when you're drunk? There's a reason for each one:

- **Your memory just... disappears:** Have you ever heard someone saying they can't remember a thing after a night out drinking? That's called a blackout. When alcohol in your blood hits a certain level, your brain literally stops recording new memories. You're still walking and talking—but your brain's "save" button is switched off.
- And if it keeps happening, the part of your brain that handles memory (the *hippocampus*) can actually shrink.
- **Coordination? What coordination?:** Have you ever seen someone walk funny after a drink or slur their words? That's alcohol messing with the connection between their brain and body by slowing down their cerebellum—the part that controls balance and coordination. It's like operating with a lag or trying to play a game with terrible Wi-Fi.
- **Impulse control has left the chat:** That little voice in your head that usually says "maybe don't send that text" or "jumping off this roof into the pool might not end well." Alcohol basically puts that voice on mute, especially during adolescence, when your brain is still developing those critical thinking skills. This is how "just

> one drink" turns into "why did I think challenging that bouncer to arm wrestle was a good idea?"

That's the brain on alcohol in real time, but the way it affects you doesn't just depend on what you drink—it's how much and how fast.

The Binge Drinking Trap

Binge drinking means slamming several drinks in a short amount of time, usually four to five within two hours. It's the classic party move: shots, chugging games, beer pong. It might look fun, but here's the problem—your body can't keep up. You're basically overloading your system before it has time to process what's already there.

And the impact isn't just temporary. Studies show that binge drinking can cause real changes in the brain: less gray matter, messed-up neural connections, and weaker communication between different parts of your brain. Translation? You're literally rewiring your brain in ways that make thinking, remembering, and emotional control harder down the line.

Then Comes the Aftermath

That next-morning hangover? It's not just your body "feeling rough." That pounding head, nausea, zero energy, and foggy thinking? That's dehydration and inflammation in your brain. And the effects don't vanish after breakfast. Hangovers can mess with your memory, your focus, and your mood for days after. It's like your brain's still trying to reboot—except half the system files are corrupted.

The Scary Part

Push past your limits, and it's not just about feeling awful the next day. Alcohol poisoning is real—and it's deadly. Your breathing slows. Your heart rate drops. In some cases, people pass out and never wake up. Add to that the increased risks of drunk driving, aggression, getting hurt, being assaulted, or developing long-term addiction, and the whole "wild night" starts to look a lot more like a trap.

The Bigger Cost

Some people talk about alcohol like it's just something you do to loosen up, fit in, or have fun. But it doesn't wait until you're older to start doing damage. It gets to work right away—right in the middle of the years when your brain is still building the systems that shape how you think, feel, move, and make decisions.

When you start drinking early, you're not just risking a hangover. You're setting yourself up for problems with memory, impulse control, mood regulation, and even addiction. And it doesn't take drinking every day to get there. A few nights of binge drinking can start changing the way your brain is wired.

So no, alcohol isn't just a phase or a harmless party trick. It's a chemical that hijacks your system, scrambles your judgment, and acts like it's your friend.

Now that you've seen how alcohol plays dirty, it's time to look at what else can pull you in and start rewiring your system without asking.

DRUGS: WHAT YOU NEED TO KNOW

You've probably heard all sorts of stuff about drugs—some of it glamorized in movies or music, some of it from that one friend who claims, "It's not that bad." The reality? Let's find out.

The "Chill" Drug That Isn't So Chill

"But it's natural!" That's the classic line about weed (marijuana). Sure, it's a plant. So is poison ivy, and you don't see people rolling that up to smoke. The fact is, weed can be addictive—despite all the "no way!" you might hear.

About 1 in 10 people who use marijuana will develop an addiction to it. If someone starts using in their teens, that risk roughly doubles to around 1 in 6. In other words, for every six teens who regularly use marijuana, one will likely become dependent on it. The risk is even higher with daily or almost daily use, taking that number up to 25–50%.

Also, this isn't your grandpa's backyard stash. THC (the part that gets you high) used to hover around 2–3% in the 70s. Now? Some strains hit 30%, and *edibles can spike over 90%*. That kind of hit can trigger panic attacks, paranoia, or even psychosis.

Party Drugs and Pills

Big party, too many people, loud music, and someone hands you a pill or line and says, "Just try it." A lot of people think it's normal. But party drugs and prescription pill misuse can go from "Wheee, this is awesome!" to "Oh no, this is *really* bad!" in a heartbeat.

What's in the Mix?

Below is a handy table of some common drugs and what they can do to you:

Drug type	Street names	What it feels	The ugly truth
Uppers (stimulants)	Coke, Molly (Ecstasy/MDMA), Speed, Addy (Adderall misuse)	Intense energy, fast talking, fast heartbeat. You feel wired and overstimulated.	The crash hits hard—think exhaustion, anxiety, and major mood swings. MDMA can overheat your body so badly that you pass out, or worse. Long-term? Heart problems and serious addiction risks.
Downers (painkillers and sedatives)	Xanax, Oxy, Percs, Vikes, Lean (codeine cough syrup)	Heavy, drowsy, slow. Pain and stress fade. You feel detached or numb.	Super addictive. Slows breathing way down—too much and you stop breathing altogether. Most street pills are laced with fentanyl, which can kill in one dose.
Psychedelics (hallucinogens and dissociatives)	Shrooms, Acid (LSD), Special K (Ketamine)	Distorted senses. Time, space, and reality feel off. Emotions swing hard.	Can mess with your head permanently—paranoia, bad trips, or even psychosis. You can't "untrip" until it wears off, no matter how bad it gets.

What It All Comes Down To

Drugs don't always look scary. Sometimes it's just a joint passed around, a half pill at a concert, or a "chill" high at someone's house. But the risks now are higher than ever. Fentanyl—one of the deadliest substances out there—isn't just hiding in sketchy street drugs. It's showing up in fake Xanax, party pills, even vapes. You can't smell it. You can't taste it. And it takes just a tiny amount to shut your body down.

If you're not 100% sure what something is or where it came from, there is no "safe" amount. One hit, one pill, one time can be all it takes. You're not just chasing a high—you're taking a bet with your brain, your body, and your life on the line.

When It Goes Too Far

A lot of people think overdose is something that happens to "other" people: the heavy users or the addicts. But overdose doesn't care if it's your first time or your fiftieth. It can hit without warning—and when it does, it hits fast.

Know the signs:

- shallow or no breathing
- blue lips or fingernails
- passed out or won't wake up
- confused, disoriented, or totally unresponsive

If you see this happening to someone—call for help, no hesitation. Many places have Good Samaritan laws that protect you from getting into trouble if you're calling 911 to help someone in an overdose situation. You could save someone's life.

VAPING AND NICOTINE: THE ADDICTION DISGUISED AS A TREND

Smoking and vaping are basically different roads leading to the same place: addiction to nicotine. Smoking and vaping might seem like two different things—cigarettes are old-school, harsh, and hard to hide.

Vapes? They feel cleaner than smoking, and it looks cleaner. No smoke cloud, no yellow teeth, no permanent stench in your hoodie. But what's inside hits your body just as hard, if not harder.

Some vape pods have more nicotine than a pack of cigarettes, and it enters your system fast. You might not even feel it until your brain starts depending on it.

Why Nicotine Hooks So Fast

Nicotine messes with your brain's reward system—the part that's still wiring itself up in your teens. A hit might feel relaxing. Maybe a little buzzy. Then your brain says, "Cool, let's do that again." And again. And again.

Before long, you're not reaching for it because not hitting it makes you feel worse. That's withdrawal, and it can hit like this:

- headaches that don't quit
- mood swings that make you snap for no reason
- brain fog that makes focusing feel impossible
- a restless craving that nothing else seems to fix

"Not as Bad" Still Isn't Safe

A lot of guys brush off the risk. "It's just vaping. Better than smoking, right?" But that logic falls apart fast.

Some of the worst lung damage that doctors are seeing right now is not from chain smokers. It comes from people who thought vaping was no big deal, like the 17-year-old who needed a double lung transplant after using vape pods for a couple of years.

We don't even know all the long-term effects of vaping yet. But what we've already seen—chronic coughs, shortness of breath, and hospital stays—isn't exactly promising.

So Why Do So Many Guys Still Do It?

It's not just the flavors or the hype. It's the way it fits into real life. You're stressed, and one hit feels like a breather. You're bored, and it gives your hands something to do. You're hanging out with friends, and everyone's passing it around—so you do too.

That's exactly what the vape companies want. They don't care if you're 14 or 40. They design these things to look cool, taste like candy, and slide right into your pocket. Because the earlier you start, the longer they've got you.

Saying no might make you feel like the odd one out. But long term, you're the one who keeps your brain sharp, your lungs strong, and your independence intact.

Now, not all habits come with smoke or clouds. Some show up in pixels, controllers, or the rush of a risky bet. Let's dig into that next.

GAMING AND GAMBLING: THE HIDDEN ADDICTIONS

Gaming is awesome. It's where you squad up, escape reality, trash-talk your friends, and maybe even feel like a legend for a bit. But there's a side most people don't talk about: how games are built to keep you playing—for profit.

Games That Play You Back

Daily log-ins, XP boosts, and battle passes are more than cool features. They're part of a system designed to lock your brain into "just one more game." Every win or unlock triggers dopamine, and your brain loves it. So it keeps chasing that hit.

What feels like fun starts turning into a hard-to-break habit. It's not technically a drug, but your brain doesn't know the difference.

Then there's the money side. Loot boxes, microtransactions, limited-time bundles, or a chance at something cool—rare gear, a skin that's gone tomorrow, or a boost you "need." Each time you don't get it, you're nudged to try again. That's the exact same psychology used in casinos.

Betting on "Easy Money"

Once real money gets involved, the game changes. Maybe it starts with a small bet on a match—just five bucks, nothing major. Then your team wins. You get that buzz. Suddenly, you're thinking, *"I could be good at this."* That buzz is bait. Whether you win or lose, your brain tells you to go again.

Gambling shows up in fantasy leagues, sports apps, online casinos, and even influencer streams hyping their "big wins." It's everywhere—and it's made to look easy.

Gaming and gambling run on the same loop: a little bit of reward, just enough to keep you chasing. So if something's starting to feel a little too sticky, it might be time to pay attention.

WHAT TO DO ABOUT IT

We've covered the major traps—alcohol, vaping, weed, harder drugs, gambling, and gaming. But knowing *what* they are is only part of the deal. How do you know when something fun starts turning into something controlling—and what can you actually do about it?

Spotting the Shift

When something that used to feel optional starts feeling like a requirement—like you're not fully okay without it—it's time to pay attention.

Maybe it starts small:

- You're staying up late with "just one more round"... for the third night in a row.
- You skip the gym or blow off plans because this one thing takes priority.
- You find yourself hiding it, brushing it off, or making excuses.
- You feel off when you don't get your usual fix—moody, edgy, distracted.

- You're thinking about it all the time, even when you're not doing it.

These are the early signs—your brain nudging you that something's off. Then there are the signs that hit harder:

- You need more to feel the same. That buzz fades, so you chase it harder.
- You've already seen consequences—bad grades, missed practices, awkward conversations—but it hasn't made you stop.
- You've tried to quit and couldn't. That's not a personal failure—it's a red flag.
- Everything else feels dull by comparison.
- You start planning your day around when and how you'll get your next hit, scroll, drink, puff, or round.

If any of that hits close to home, it means you've got a chance to do something different—starting now.

How to Quit (and Actually Stay Quit)

Addiction doesn't always show up with a dramatic rock bottom. Sometimes it's just you, stuck in a loop you didn't notice at first—until it started calling the shots. Here's how to start flipping the script:

- **Name what's happening:** Addiction feeds on denial. So, first move? Call it what it is. "I'm addicted." "This has too much control over me." That sentence might feel weird to say, but naming it makes it real and beatable.

- **Pick a quit day:** "Someday" always slips. Choose a real date. Write it down. Tell someone. Now it's not just a wish—it's a plan you've committed to.
- **Swap the habit:** When you remove the hit, you need to train your brain to get dopamine somewhere else. Exercise, music, learning a new skill, skateboarding, even solving puzzles—it's about creating a new feedback loop that keeps your reward system engaged without pulling you under.
- **Change your environment:** Addictions have favorite hangouts. The vape spot is behind the gym. The phone scrolls after midnight. The friend group that always lights up at parties. You don't have to ditch your life, but switching up routines helps more than you think. Distance makes space for better choices.
- **Build your team:** You weren't built to do this solo. You need at least one person who knows you're trying to quit—someone who'll check in, not check out. Could be a friend, a sibling, a coach, or your mom (yeah, really). If things feel bigger than that? Therapy and support groups are real tools, not just stuff for people on TV.
- **Push through the hard part:** Depending on what you're quitting, your brain might throw a full tantrum. Cravings. Mood swings. Trouble sleeping. Irritation over everything and nothing. That's your brain adjusting. Most of those symptoms fade within 5–10 days. Stay with it. The fog lifts.
- **Track real wins:** First full day without a vape? Win. Left the party early instead of getting roped into something dumb? Win. It all proofs that change is happening, even if it feels slow.

If You Need Help, You're Not Alone

Addiction thrives in isolation. That's why one of the most effective ways to break it is by doing the opposite—getting connected. Groups like Narcotics Anonymous (NA) and Alcoholics Anonymous (AA) work because you're surrounded by people who've been there. You share the struggle, hold each other accountable, and remind each other it's possible to change. Recovery works better in a community. Always has.

Therapy can help, too—especially when you want to understand the deeper "why" behind your habits. It's not just about quitting. It's about healing what made you reach for the substance or behavior in the first place.

In crisis? Reach out. In the U.S., call or text 988 for the Suicide & Crisis Lifeline. In the U.K., contact 0800 58 58 58 (for young men via CALM) or 0800 1111 (Childline, under 19). These are free, confidential, and open 24/7.

You're not weak for needing help. You're human. Asking for support means you're done living stuck, and ready to take your life back.

How to Say No in the Moment

After everything we've covered, it helps to have a few go to move when you don't want to mess with substances—or you're trying to quit—without feeling like the odd one out. Pressure happens, but you can stay solid without making it awkward.

- **Keep it short and confident:** "I'm good." "Nah, not for me." You don't owe a speech. Chill confidence says more than any excuse.

- **Have a solid excuse ready:** "Big game tomorrow." "Don't want to mess with my focus." "Already had a rough week." These lands, and most people won't push back.
- **Bring backup:** Rolling with someone else who's also skipping it makes it easier to hold your ground. A look. A nod. Instant support.
- **Changed your mind? That's allowed:** Even if you said yes five minutes ago, you can still say, "Actually, I'm done." No shame in walking it back.

The moment when you choose what's right for you is where real control starts.

THE POWER OF CHOICE

Addiction doesn't care how smart you are or what your plans look like—it can sneak in before you realize what's happening. But once you understand how it works, you've got something powerful: choice.

And choice matters, especially when the next move could come with real consequences. So let's break down the other risks waiting in the mix—and what they can cost you.

FOURTEEN

GOOD DECISIONS VS BAD DECISIONS

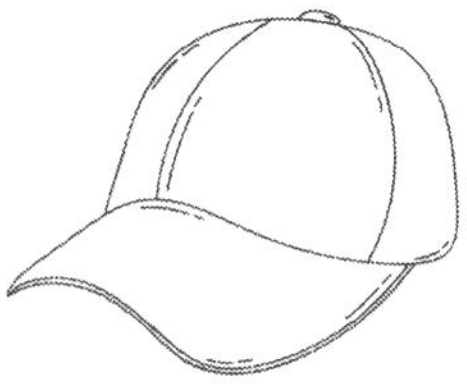

Risk has a pull—no denying it. That little "What if..." spark shows up when you're eyeing the top of a half-pipe, thinking about jumping off that bridge into the river, or hyping yourself up to ask your crush to hang out. It's the rush. The edge. The moment that feels like anything could happen.

And weirdly? Your brain is built for it.

YOUR BRAIN IS A RISK-TAKING MACHINE (BY DESIGN)

Risk-taking isn't some glitch in your teen years—it's your brain doing exactly what it's designed to do. For a long time, researchers thought teens made bad decisions because they lacked self-control. Now we know better: your brain is learning how the world works through firsthand experience.

During adolescence, the part of your brain that lights up for rewards—the ventral striatum—is in overdrive, basically yelling "Go for it!" anytime something exciting crosses your path. Meanwhile, your prefrontal cortex—the part that handles logic, caution, and long-term thinking—is still wiring itself up.

The result? A brain that craves intense, rewarding experiences but is still learning how to tell the difference between a good idea and a disaster with a soundtrack.

Most of the time, it's not that you lack control—it's that you don't have enough experience yet. So your brain pushes you to try stuff, gather feedback, and figure out what works. That's how you grow.

Why Risk-Taking Actually Makes Sense

That buzz you get before landing a trick, sending a bold text, or trying something new? That's your brain releasing dopamine and adrenaline—natural fuel for bold moves and growth.

Here's what's really driving it:

- **Exploration mode:** You're testing your limits, figuring out what you're capable of.
- **Stress release:** Sometimes, taking a leap feels like breathing again.
- **Boredom buster:** Routine can feel like a flatline; risk brings the spike.
- **Connection:** Wild moments with friends can make you feel understood, even without words.
- **Identity formation:** Every challenge shapes who you're becoming.
- **Proving ground:** Some risks are about showing off. Others are about proving something real to yourself.

Now toss your friends into the mix. When they're around—or even just watching online—your brain's reward system dials up to max. That's why the "what if" gets louder, and the "maybe don't" barely gets a word in. Your brain actually processes rewards differently when peers are in the picture.

The Bottom Line

Every time you push a boundary, you're not just being impulsive—you're gathering data. Your brain is constantly asking: *Can I handle this? Is it worth it? What makes me feel alive?*

Sometimes you'll stick the landing. Sometimes you'll wipe out. Both teach you something important.

You don't need to shut down your adventurous streak. You just need to learn how to spot the difference between a risk that helps you grow... and one that starts with "watch this" and ends in the ER —or worse.

MINOR AND MAJOR CRIMES: UNDERSTANDING THE LINE

That same wiring can lead you straight into trouble. In fact, statistics show that around 80% of young guys commit some kind of crime by the time they're 24. Guys aged 18 to 25 alone make up about a quarter of all arrests in the U.S.

Part of the reason? Society tells boys to "man up," be bold, aggressive, and adventurous. That's not always bad, but sometimes it translates into reckless decisions. Another big factor is your environment. If your crew shrugs off or even celebrates bad behavior, you're way more likely to follow along.

Because it doesn't take a grand plan to break the law, let's get clear about which minor moves can become big problems, and which choices can straight-up nuke your future.

Minor League Mess-Ups

Most crimes teens get caught up in are impulsive, messy, and over in seconds. A dumb dare, a "harmless" thrill, something you thought wouldn't matter. But even small mistakes can lead to big problems: fines, community service, or a permanent record. That five-second laugh suddenly isn't funny.

Here are some of the usual suspects:

- **Underage drinking or weed possession:** Maybe you're thinking, "It's just a party, everyone's drinking," or "It's just weed." But underage drinking and possession aren't just frowned upon—they're illegal everywhere. Even if it's your first time, you might face fines, probation (meaning regular check-ins with the court), mandatory drug or alcohol classes, or even temporarily losing your driver's license.
- **Shoplifting:** Snagging a candy bar might seem harmless or funny in the moment. But stores don't laugh. Most have security cameras and a zero-tolerance policy, no matter how small the item. Retail theft often leads to fines, community service (cleaning parks, volunteering), or a requirement to complete theft-awareness classes. Plus, getting banned from your favorite stores can be more embarrassing than getting caught.
- **Vandalism:** Spray-painting a wall or smashing a window might feel like rebellious fun—until the bill for damages arrives. Vandalism often means paying for repairs, sometimes hundreds or thousands of dollars out of your own or your family's pocket. You might also end up doing community service.

Reckless Driving and Speeding

Cars deserve special attention because behind the wheel, small mistakes turn major quickly.

Speeding normally starts with that surge of power—engine roaring, friends cheering, road wide open. It feels like a flex... until it crashes into reality.

Car crashes are the second leading cause of death for teenagers. Teens are more likely to speed, less likely to wear seatbelts, and easily distracted, especially with friends in the car. Add alcohol or weed, and you have a disaster waiting to happen.

Even if you're not driving, you're still responsible. Here's how to avoid a deadly ride:

- **Stay focused:** Phones and driving don't mix. Sending a single text takes your eyes off the road for around five seconds—at highway speeds, that's like driving across a football field blindfolded. Keep your phone out of reach.
- **Don't tailgate:** Following too close to the car ahead doesn't make them speed up—it makes your chance of crashing skyrocket. Keep at least a three-second space. Count slowly to three from when the car ahead passes a sign—then you should pass it. That space could save your life.
- **Limit passengers:** The more passengers in your car, especially friends your age, the higher your crash risk. Teens with two or more passengers are three times likelier to crash. Limit passengers and set clear boundaries for behavior.
- **Drive sober or don't drive:** Even small amounts of alcohol or weed impair your reaction time, coordination, and judgment. About 25% of fatal teen crashes involve

alcohol. Calling for a sober ride or walking home beats causing serious injury—or worse.

A minor crime might not send you to juvie, but it still sticks. Records can disrupt college applications, job opportunities, or even apartment rentals. One impulsive decision can follow you way longer than you intended.

Major League Crimes

Some crimes go beyond minor slips. They seriously damage lives, including yours. These are the big-league offenses—serious mistakes with consequences you can't erase.

- **Breaking and entering (Burglary):** Breaking into someone's home, garage, or even their car to steal things isn't just stealing—it's called burglary, and it's serious. Burglary is a felony, meaning it's a crime serious enough to land you in state prison, not just juvenile detention. A felony on your record makes getting jobs or even renting apartments extremely difficult. "Just grabbing something quick" isn't worth losing your freedom.
- **Drug dealing:** Selling weed, pills, or other drugs might seem like easy money. But getting caught dealing is a felony. Drug charges come with heavy consequences, including jail sentences measured in years, not days. Even first-time offenders can end up behind bars. Selling even a small amount can label you as a drug dealer for life.
- **Physical assault:** Getting into a fight seems common enough—until someone gets seriously hurt. If your punches cause serious injury, what you thought was a

fight becomes aggravated assault, another felony. That means potential prison time and huge fines. It also means facing lawsuits from the victim, hospital bills, and carrying a violent offender label forever.

- **Sexual assault:** Ignoring consent, pushing someone sexually, or crossing clear boundaries is never minor. Sexual assault is prosecuted as a felony in most cases, bringing severe punishment, jail sentences, and mandatory lifelong registration as a sex offender. That record never goes away, restricting where you live, work, or study.

CHOICES BUILD FUTURES

So, where does all this leave you? With a choice. You can dodge responsibility, let consequences pile up, and hope for the best. Or, you can take accountability, own your story, and steer it in the direction you want.

Before we move into the next chapter, let's pressure-test these new skills. The quick quiz up next will show you which instincts are solid and which ones still need training.

QUIZ: DANGER ZONE DECODER

Answer each question with the choice that feels right. When you're done, flip to the answer key at the back of the book and see how you scored.

1. **Which brain chemical creates the "rush" that addictive habits and substances hijack?**
   a. Serotonin
   b. Dopamine
   c. Melatonin
2. **How does alcohol really affect a teen's brain?**
   a. It boosts memory formation
   b. It slows brain development and weakens decision-making
   c. It has no long-term impact if you only drink on weekends
3. **Vaping feels cleaner than smoking, yet it's still highly addictive because:**
   a. Most vape pods are nicotine-free
   b. Marketing makes it look harmless, but the nicotine dose hits the brain fast
   c. Vapor is just flavored water
4. **What counts as binge drinking for a teen boy?**
   a. Two alcoholic drinks in an evening
   b. Five or more drinks in about two hours
   c. Any alcohol before age 18
5. **Which behavior warns that gaming may be turning into an addiction?**
   a. Weekend practice sessions to improve skills
   b. Skipping sleep, school, or friends to keep playing

   c. Watching esports streams at lunch

6. **A friend calls you "boring" for refusing a pill. What's the smart first move?**
   a. Take half to keep the peace
   b. Say, "No thanks, I'm good," and change the subject
   c. Walk away without a word
7. **Underage drinking or weed possession is labeled in the book as:**
   a. A major-league crime
   b. A minor-league mess-up that still brings real consequences
   c. Not illegal if everyone does it
8. **When quitting feels impossible, the book recommends:**
   a. Going cold turkey in secret
   b. Reaching out to counselors, hotlines, or trusted adults
   c. Doubling the habit to build tolerance

PART FIVE
BECOMING MY BEST SELF

FIFTEEN
DISCOVERING ME

Becoming the best version of yourself starts with understanding who you are. That means getting a feel for your personality, your habits, what drains you, and what drives you. Once you get how you operate, decisions make more sense, and confidence shows up without forcing it.

So, where do you begin? One way is by noticing how you handle pressure, people, and the stuff that throws you off. The quick personality quiz below is here to help with that.

Let's see where you land.

QUICK PERSONALITY CHECK-IN

Pick the answer that feels most like you. No overthinking—just go with what makes sense.

1. When you get handed a surprise group assignment, you usually...

1. Jump in with a plan and start assigning tasks.

2. Wait to see what others do, then quietly take the part you're best at.
3. Try to get everyone involved, so the group feels balanced.
4. Suggest everyone work solo and combine their work later.

2. You're invited to a party where you barely know anyone. Your first thought?

1. Let's go—it's a chance to meet people and maybe take over the playlist.
2. I'll go if someone I trust is there, otherwise probably not.
3. I'll check it out, but I'll be hanging in the corner unless it gets interesting.
4. Hard pass—I'd rather use that time for something I actually enjoy.

3. A heated debate breaks out in class. What do you do?

1. Jump in. You've got opinions and don't mind defending them.
2. Wait, listen, then add your take if it seems worth it.
3. Step in if things get out of hand—you'd rather keep the peace.
4. Stay out of it completely. Drama drains you.

4. When a big decision lands in your lap, your go-to move is:

1. Act fast—you trust your gut.

2. Gather facts and think it through.
3. Ask around and talk it out.
4. Step back and process alone before doing anything.

5. Free time finally opens up. You're most likely to:

1. Start something new—project, plan, adventure, whatever.
2. Dive deeper into a current interest or hobby.
3. Catch up with people you've been meaning to check in on.
4. Chill completely—zero expectations, just recharge.

WHAT YOUR ANSWERS SAY ABOUT YOU

You probably didn't answer all 1's or all 3's—that's the point. Most people are a mix. But the pattern you lean toward can show you something useful about how you operate and how you interact with the world.

Mostly 1's: The Driver

You're action-oriented, energetic, and not afraid to take the lead. You like movement, challenge, and results, and you tend to trust your gut when making decisions. People probably see you as bold and confident, even if you don't always feel that way inside. Just remember: slowing down sometimes gives you more control, not less. You don't have to act fast to be strong.

Mostly 2's: The Analyzer

You think things through, take your time, and usually have a game plan—whether you say it out loud or not. You notice details that other people miss, and you'd rather be precise than impulsive. You're probably the one others rely on when things get chaotic. Just watch out for overthinking or hesitation. Progress beats perfection.

Mostly 3's: The Connector

You're relationship-focused, tuned in to what people feel, and often the one holding the group together. Whether you realize it or not, you've got emotional radar—which can be a superpower. You care about harmony, and people trust you. Just make sure you don't shrink your own needs just to keep the peace. Your voice matters too.

Mostly 4's: The Independent

You like space, clarity, and time to think. You're probably more low-key than loud, and you're not into doing things just because everyone else is. You've got strong internal standards, and when you choose to do something, it's because it *means* something to you. Just stay aware of when isolation turns into avoidance—you don't have to do it all alone.

None of these styles is better or worse—they just shape how you see the world and move through it.

YOUR VALUES

Now that you've got a feel for how you tend to operate, it's time to figure out *why* you move the way you do.

A lot of people think morals and values mean the same thing, but they don't. Morals are your sense of right and wrong—what feels fair, respectful, or safe across the board. You don't have to be taught that hurting people, stealing, or lying feels wrong. That's your moral compass at work.

Values are personal. They're what matters most to *you*. Not just what's right, but what's important. You and your friend might both agree that cheating is wrong (morals), but you might value honesty more while they value loyalty—so you'd handle the situation differently.

Knowing the difference helps to keep you from getting steamrolled in situations where you feel conflicted or pressured to go along with something that doesn't sit right. While giving you a sense of stability, you can lean on it when things around you get messy.

How Do You Figure Out Your Values?

You probably don't walk around thinking, *"Respect and loyalty are guiding my every move."* But you do feel it when something rubs you the wrong way. You sense it when you speak up for someone who's being treated unfairly—or when you feel like you've crossed a line and it doesn't sit right. That's your values kicking in.

So, how do you figure them out? You don't overthink it. You notice what you're drawn to, what you push back against, and what kind of people you actually respect.

Here's a quick check-in. Pick 3–5 values that feel real to you, not just what sounds impressive:

- loyalty
- honesty
- freedom
- growth

- creativity
- respect
- responsibility
- kindness
- courage
- justice
- curiosity
- integrity
- compassion

So What Now?

Your values shape everything: how you make decisions, how you show up, and how you grow. They're tools:

- **When you're making a tough call:** Values help you choose what actually feels right, not just what's easy or expected.
- **When you set goals:** They help you focus on what matters to *you*—not just what looks good on paper.
- **When you're around other people:** Shared values create a real connection.
- **When something feels off:** Your values are often the reason why.
- **When you're building confidence:** Values give you stability. You don't have to fake it when you know what you stand for.

So don't just choose your values—use them:

- If you picked *discipline*, try setting a personal rule you actually stick to—like silencing your phone during homework or showing up on time even when no one else does.

- If you choose *creativity*, don't wait for the "perfect idea." Make something messy. Write a random verse. Build in Minecraft. Sketch what's in your head. It doesn't have to be deep—it just has to be yours.
- If *respect* made your list, check how you talk to people, especially when you're annoyed. Real respect shows up in tone, timing, and when you listen without waiting to fire back.
- If you value *loyalty*, show up when it counts—not just when it's convenient. Stick with your people, even when it's hard, but don't lose yourself in the process.
- If *honesty* stands out to you, practice it in moments where stretching the truth would be easier, like owning a mistake before anyone catches it, or telling a friend what they need to hear, not just what they want to.
- If you picked *curiosity*, follow it. Ask the extra question. Dig deeper. Try stuff you've never done before, even if you're bad at it. Curiosity grows your world.
- If you're drawn to *kindness*, don't wait for the "right" time to use it. Hold the door. DM someone who's having a rough day. Be decent even when no one's watching.

That's how you stop getting pushed around by everything outside you—and start being led by what's solid inside.

GROWTH MINDSET: UPGRADING HOW YOU THINK

Once you know more about who you are and how you think, the next step is to adopt a growth mindset.

A growth mindset is the belief that your abilities can improve through effort, learning, and time. It's what lets you see failure as part of the process instead of the end of the road.

Here's what it actually does:

- **It builds resilience:** You're more likely to bounce back instead of shutting down when things go wrong.
- **It keeps you motivated:** You're more willing to practice, learn, and push through the tough stuff.
- **It boosts learning:** You stay open to new info, ask better questions, and actually absorb more.
- **It helps relationships:** You become more open-minded and less stuck on being right all the time.
- **It fuels self-improvement:** You're better at adapting and growing through change instead of fighting it.

On the flip side, a fixed mindset is that voice whispering, "I'm just bad at this," or "Why even bother if I'll mess up?" It shows up whenever you hit a wall or compare yourself to someone who seems light-years ahead—and it wants you to throw in the towel before you even get started.

Choosing a growth mindset won't make everything easier, but it will make progress possible.

The Real Shape of Progress

Now, progress doesn't move in a straight line. Some weeks, you'll feel locked in and on fire. Other weeks, you'll feel distracted, discouraged, or like you're starting from scratch again.

None of that means you're failing. It just means you're doing something real.

- Say you stay up too late after promising yourself you'd fix your sleep. Don't spiral. Try again the next night.
- Say you challenge yourself to speak up in class and totally blank. That's still progress, because you tried.
- Say you want to be more present with friends, but catch yourself glued to your phone. Noticing that moment is already a win.

Improvement in the resets, in the moments you could've given up—but didn't.

WHY GOALS MATTER

Goals take all that knowledge about yourself and help you turn it into focused action. They give your time, energy, and effort somewhere to go, so you're not just drifting through your days but actually building something.

When you set a goal, you're deciding what matters to you. That choice alone helps you focus, push through the boring stuff, and keep going when things get tough. Goals also give you a way to measure progress—not just in trophies or test scores, but in growth, effort, and follow-through.

Some goals are short-term. They're like quick missions: things you can accomplish in days or weeks. Think about passing your next test, sticking to a sleep schedule, or saving enough to buy something you've had your eye on.

Other goals are long-term—the kind that take more planning, patience, and persistence. Getting into a specific school, starting a side hustle, getting stronger at a sport, or learning a language. These take time, but every move you make gets you closer.

The SMART Method

So, how do you set goals that actually work? Meet SMART goals. They're not just smart as in clever—they're an entire method to make your dreams more than just wishful thinking.

SMART stands for:

- **Specific:** Be clear about what you want. Instead of saying, "I want better grades," try, "I want to raise my math grade to an A by the end of the semester."
- **Measurable:** Track your progress. How will you know you're succeeding? With our math example, you might say, "I'll review one chapter each week."
- **Achievable:** Keep it realistic. If you're struggling with math, aiming for an A might be a stretch, but a B+ could be totally doable.
- **Relevant:** Make sure the goal aligns with what matters to you. If math is key to your dream of becoming an engineer, that A or B+ is relevant.
- **Time-Bound:** Set a deadline. "By the end of the semester" gives you a clear timeline to work toward.

How to Do It

Let's put this into action. Say your goal is to save $100 for a new gaming headset.

- **Specific:** "I want to save $100 for a headset."
- **Measurable:** "I'll save $25 a week."
- **Achievable:** "I'll cut back on buying snacks after school."

- **Relevant:** "Gaming is how I unwind and connect with friends."
- **Time-Bound:** "I'll have the money saved in four weeks."

Every piece fits, giving you a roadmap to follow. And when you hit that goal? Satisfaction.

BUILD YOUR GOAL GAME

So, what's one thing you want to make happen this month? Or this year? Doesn't have to be massive. It could be finally sticking to a routine, making the team, raising a grade, or saving up for something that matters to you. Whatever it is, break it down, write it out, and give it the SMART treatment. One step at a time. One win at a time.

When your goals match what matters to you—and fit how you naturally work—they stop feeling like pressure and start feeling like purpose. Add a growth mindset, and you're not just chasing results. You're becoming someone who keeps showing up and follows through.

That brings us to the next big piece: decision-making. Goals give you direction. Decisions determine how you get there. Let's talk about what makes a choice smart, shaky, or straight-up risky—and how to tell the difference in real time.

SIXTEEN

GOOD DECISIONS VS BAD DECISIONS

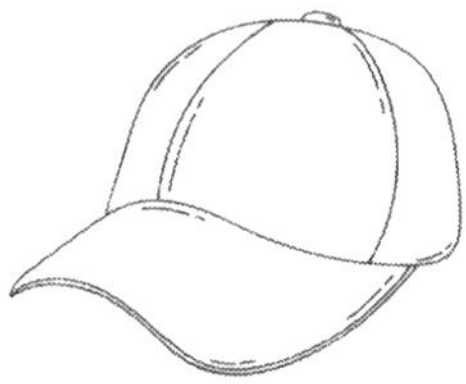

Every decision you make leaves a mark—not just on your day, but on the version of you that's slowly taking shape. Some of those choices seem small—like hitting snooze or skipping breakfast—but others shape your relationships, impact your well-being, or define who you'll become.

So, what makes a good decision? It's one that keeps you in the driver's seat, making the choice truly feel like your own. These moves typically bring you clarity, strengthen your connections, and help you make progress.

A bad choice, on the other hand, often leaves you feeling out of control or wishing you'd done something different. They can quietly shut down your confidence, limit your options, or erode your sense of control. Learning to consistently make those "good" moves and skillfully handle the "bad" ones is a skill that can change your whole game.

THE THREE C'S OF DECISION-MAKING

When life throws you a curveball, and you're faced with a tough choice or a chaotic situation, it's natural to feel the urge to react without thinking. But what if there were a way to slow down, gain control, and make choices you truly feel good about? That's exactly what the Three C's help with. Here's how it works:

Clarify

Before you even think about making a move, be clear about what's actually happening. Not what it feels like, not what you're afraid it means—just the facts.

When you're caught in a high-pressure situation—someone dares you, the group chat explodes, or you're put on the spot—your brain starts reacting before you've even processed what's going on. Clarifying slows things down just enough to figure out what you're really dealing with.

Ask yourself:

- **What exactly is happening right now?** Describe it like you're an outside observer. For example: "Someone made a joke about a teacher." "The group chat just turned mean." "They want me to skip class." Stick to the facts, not the drama.
- **Why does this feel urgent?** Is it the crowd? The pressure? A fear of being judged? Clarifying means naming the push—not letting it shove you around.

You're not trying to overanalyze; you're just trying to see the situation for what it is.

Consider

Once you're clear about what's happening, the next move is to think it through to see where it might go.

This is where you weigh the trade-offs—not in a dramatic, life-or-death way, but in a "how will this actually play out" kind of way. You're not looking for a perfect answer; you're just checking the range of possibilities before you hit go.

Ask yourself:

- What's the best thing that could come out of this?
- What's the worst thing that could happen, and could I deal with it?
- Will this still seem worth it tomorrow, or will I be trying to explain it?
- Who else could this affect—whether they're part of it or not?

Let's say you're thinking about skipping school with friends. Best case: you don't get caught, you make a memory. Worst case: you tank your attendance, lose credit, or break trust with someone who had your back. The short-term thrill might not hold up against the longer-term fallout. That's the kind of trade-off worth noticing.

Choose

After you've taken the time to understand what's really going on and thought through the potential outcomes, there's one thing left to do: choose.

- Sometimes choosing means taking action:
    - Stepping in when something crosses a line

    - Saying something that feels risky but necessary.
- Other times, it means pulling back:
    - Deciding not to respond to a message that's baiting you
    - Not showing up to something that doesn't sit right
    - Walking away before a situation turns into something you can't undo.

Here, you are not looking for a perfect answer. What you want is to make a decision you can stand by. One that isn't driven by fear, shaped by pressure, or followed by regret.

The more you practice this, the stronger your decision-making gets. Not perfect, not rigid—just clearer and more aligned with who you're trying to become.

When It Doesn't Feel So Simple

Of course, not every decision fits neatly into a process. Some situations hit harder. They're more emotional, more complicated, or tangled up in relationships, pressure, and uncertainty. That's where the Three C's still work—but they might need backup.

Ask yourself:

- Whose voice is loudest right now? Is this your decision—or is someone else steering it for you?
- Will this move you toward the life you want—or pull you in the opposite direction?
- Who can help you zoom out? A parent, coach, counselor, or older sibling might see angles you can't when you're in the thick of it.

Asking those extra questions is next-level awareness. It means you're not just reacting—you're steering.

WHAT HAPPENS WHEN YOU DON'T GET IT RIGHT

Let's talk about that gut-drop moment when you realize you've messed up. Maybe it's a missed deadline, a heated argument with someone you care about, an impulsive post you regret, or an "experiment" that went wrong. The first instinct is usually to either ignore it and hope it fades away or to spiral into a pit of regret and self-blame. Neither approach helps.

Step 1: Call It What It Is

Not what you *meant* to do. Not what *someone else* pushed you into. Just the actual move you made.

- "I broke someone's trust."
- "I backed out when someone needed support."
- "I crossed a line because I wanted to impress people."

That kind of honesty takes guts. But it also gives you control. Because now you're not hiding, defending, or spinning—you're dealing with what's real.

Step 2: Understand the Fallout

Once you've named what happened, take a look at what it caused. Did your actions hurt someone, damage a relationship, or create a ripple effect that left people cleaning up after you? Even if it didn't seem like a huge deal in the moment, that doesn't mean it didn't leave a mark.

This part isn't about feeling worse. It's about being responsible for the impact, which is the only way to earn back trust and self-respect.

Step 3: Move Toward Repair

You can't erase what happened—but you can respond with intention.

- **Say it out loud:** "I messed up, and I want to make it right."
- **Drop the excuses:** Own it without deflecting.
- **Ask what's needed:** "How can I fix this?" Or if that's not possible: "I'll do better next time, and here's how."

Real apologies don't need grand speeches. They need follow-through. They show people you're serious about changing.

Step 4: Learn the Pattern

If you stop here, you'll probably repeat the same mistake in a different form later. That's what most people do.

But if you want to level up, ask: Why did I make that decision? Were you trying to look tough? Avoid conflict? Escape stress? Get attention? Go numb?

Whatever the reason, knowing it gives you leverage. Because next time something similar shows up, you'll see the pattern before it repeats. That's what growth looks like—not just reacting differently, but *thinking* differently.

Step 5: Don't Stay Stuck

One of the hardest parts of messing up is forgiving yourself. That nagging inner voice that won't let you move on, constantly replaying the mistake? It's wrong. The truth is, everyone screws up and how you bounce back is what matters most.

So, take responsibility, learn the lesson, and then let it go. Carrying guilt only weighs you down, drains your energy, and blocks you from making better choices ahead. Forgiving yourself allows you to reset and focus on what's next.

MESS → FIX → GROW

The beauty of bad decisions is that they're temporary. Each one is a chance to reset, improve, and level up. Maybe your next move is about rebuilding trust, trying harder in school or sports, making healthier choices with your body and mind, or just making sure you don't repeat the same mistake.

And yeah, some days are going to feel off. You'll hit roadblocks, doubt yourself, or feel like nothing's clicking. That doesn't mean you're broken. It just means you're human. Next up, we'll get into those messy moods, overwhelming days, and what to do when it feels like everything's too much, because making sense of your mind is just as important as setting goals with it.

SEVENTEEN
TEEN ANGST

Being a teen can feel like having ten tabs open in your brain. Your body's changing, your brain's still wiring up, and suddenly the world expects you to figure everything out while handling school, friendships, and pressure from every direction. It's a lot.

Some days, you're buzzing with energy and can't sit still. Other days, it's like someone unplugged you from the wall. You might feel on edge, zoned out, angry for no clear reason, or like the smallest thing could tip everything over. That emotional overload? That's what people call teen angst—and it's way more common than anyone admits out loud.

Let's break down the three major moods that show up when life gets heavy and how to respond when they hit.

ANXIETY: WHEN EVERYTHING FEELS LIKE TOO MUCH

Anxiety feels like... and it doesn't always show up as panic attacks or full-blown meltdowns. Sometimes it sneaks in like background noise that keeps getting louder until you can no longer focus on anything else.

You might recognize it as the pressure to keep up, the fear of saying the wrong thing, or the loop of "what ifs" that won't leave you alone. It can feel like dread, even when nothing obvious is going wrong—like your brain's running a race your body didn't sign up for.

What It Feels Like in the Body

Anxiety has a way of showing up all over your body, even if you don't realize it at first.

- Your chest might feel tight, like it's harder to breathe.
- Your heart might race, even if you're not moving.
- Your stomach could twist into a nervous pit.
- You might feel fidgety, jumpy, or like you need to escape, but don't know where to go.
- Your muscles might feel tense, your shoulders creeping up toward your ears.

Sometimes, you don't even realize you're anxious until your body tells you first. It's like your nervous system hits the panic button before your brain figures out why.

What Sets It Off

There's no single cause of anxiety, but a few patterns tend to show up during the teen years. Things are shifting fast, expectations rise, and your brain is still wiring itself.. So it makes sense that some days feel overwhelming.

Here are some common triggers:

- **Social pressure:** Feeling like you have to say the right thing, wear the right thing, or be liked by the right people.
- **Performance stress:** Grades, sports, auditions, tryouts—anything where you're being judged or evaluated can crank up the pressure.
- **Uncertainty:** Not knowing what's going to happen, whether that's about plans changing or big life stuff like your future, can make you feel like the ground isn't steady.
- **Comparing yourself:** Whether it's on social media or in real life, constantly measuring yourself against others is a fast track to feeling like you're falling behind.
- **Trying to do it all:** You may not want to disappoint anyone—friends, parents, coaches, teachers—but trying to be everything to everyone leaves zero room to breathe.

Even small things can stack up until your system gets overloaded.

What Helps

The goal isn't to make anxiety disappear completely. That's not realistic, and sometimes anxiety is actually useful (like when it reminds you to prepare for a test or be cautious in a sketchy situation). The goal is to recognize when it's taking over and know how to bring it down to a manageable level.

Here's what can help:

1. **Breathe—seriously:** It sounds too simple, but slowing down your breath tells your brain that you're not in danger. Try this: Breathe in for 4 seconds, hold for 4,

out for 4, pause for 4. Do that a few times. Your body listens to your breath more than your thoughts.

2. **Say it to yourself:** "I feel anxious." That small moment of naming it creates space between you and the feeling. You're not anxiety—you're a person *feeling* anxiety. That helps make it less overwhelming.
3. **Move your body:** Walk, stretch, do push-ups and dance around your room. Anxiety builds energy—it needs somewhere to go. Physical movement helps your nervous system release the tension it's been holding onto.
4. **Play calming sounds:** Soothing music, nature sounds, or ambient noise can interrupt the spiral. It's not just background—your brain takes cues from sound. Quiet music = calm brain. YouTube and Spotify are packed with playlists that do the job.
5. **Try a short meditation:** You don't need to be a monk. Apps like Headspace, Insight Timer, or even a simple YouTube video can walk you through a five-minute reset. The goal isn't to "clear your mind"—it's to come back to the present, one breath at a time.
6. **Get out of your head:** Anxiety loves to trap you in your thoughts. Break the loop by getting into something physical or sensory. Chew ice. Splash cold water on your face. Focus on five things you can see, four you can touch, three you can hear, two you can smell, one you can taste. It grounds you.
7. **Reframe the story:** Instead of "What if I fail?" try "What if I figure it out?" Instead of "Everyone's going to think I'm awkward," try "Most people are too busy thinking about themselves to notice." Your brain believes the stories you repeat. Pick better ones.

8. **Talk to someone:** You don't have to explain everything perfectly. Simply saying, "I've been feeling off lately," can be enough to initiate the conversation. Anxiety loves isolation. Talking breaks that pattern.

You don't need to fight it. You just need to notice it, respond with care, and trust that it will pass, because it will.

ANGER: WHEN EVERYTHING BOILS OVER

Anger itself isn't bad. It's not something to be ashamed of. It's just one of the ways your brain signals that something feels wrong, unfair, or out of control. Sometimes it explodes. Sometimes it simmers just under the surface—like a pressure cooker with no release valve.

What It Feels Like in the Body

You might notice

- your heart pounding or your chest tightening
- muscles tensing—especially your jaw, shoulders, or hands
- heat rushing to your face or ears
- a strong urge to do something, *anything*, just to let it out

Your body is prepping for fight mode. But most of the time, the "danger" you're reacting to isn't a life-or-death situation.

Where It Comes From

Anger usually doesn't show up by itself. It rides in with other emotions that are harder to admit or harder to deal with. Stuff like:

- feeling disrespected
- being misunderstood or ignored
- feeling powerless or embarrassed
- trying to protect someone you care about
- feeling like you're constantly being pushed, tested, or provoked

In a way, anger is like the armor your brain throws on to protect something more vulnerable underneath. It's easier to say "I'm pissed off" than "I'm scared," "I'm hurt," or "I feel out of control."

Sometimes it's triggered by something small, but the emotion is big because it's built on other things you've been holding in. Anger stacks. If you never get to let it out in healthy ways, it piles up until the next thing—no matter how minor—tips it over.

What Helps

You don't need to stop feeling angry. You just need to find ways to work with it, not against it.

1. **Catch it early:** Anger moves fast, but there's usually a second—just one—where you can notice it coming on. Your fists clench. Your voice gets louder. Your face gets hot. If you can catch it in that moment, you've got options.
2. **Take space, not revenge:** Walking away isn't weak. It's one of the strongest things you can do when your

emotions are about to wreck your relationships, your reps, or your day. Cool down first. Then decide what action—if any—needs to happen.

3. **Give your body a release:** Anger is also physical. You need to move. Go for a run. Hit a pillow. Do push-ups until you can't anymore. Sprint down the block. Energy that builds has to go somewhere. Choose where it lands.
4. **Ask yourself:** What's underneath this? Did someone cross a boundary? Did I feel embarrassed? Was I already stressed, and this just made it worse? Even saying, "I'm not just mad—I'm hurt," helps your brain calm down and process instead of just exploding.
5. **Talk it out once you're calm:** Anger usually means a boundary was crossed. Once you've calmed down, speak clearly. Say what bothered you and why. Don't attack—explain. It's the difference between creating change and starting drama.
6. **Learn your patterns**: Do you always lose it when you feel disrespected? When do people interrupt you? When does someone lie? The more you know what sets you off, the better you get at spotting it early and responding in ways you won't regret.

Anger isn't the enemy. It's information. It shows you what matters to you, what you're protecting, and where you might need to draw a clearer line.

The goal isn't to be less angry—it's to be more in charge of how you use it. Controlled anger can speak up for you, defend you, and push you to change things that feel unfair. Out-of-control anger? That's the stuff that burns bridges and leaves messes behind.

Now let's talk about the other side of the emotional spectrum—

when it's not fire but fog. When you're not overwhelmed by *too much* feeling, but by almost none at all.

SHUTDOWN: WHEN YOU JUST STOP CARING

Not every reaction is loud. Sometimes, the way your mind responds to stress or pressure is by turning the volume all the way down.

You might catch yourself saying, *"I don't care,"* or *"Whatever,"* or *"It doesn't matter."* And maybe you believe it, or maybe it's just the only thing you have the energy left to say.

The truth is, it does matter. But something in you has hit pause because it feels like too much to deal with.

What It Feels Like

Shutdown feels like dragging through your day with the lights on, but nobody home. You might feel:

- tired for no clear reason
- mentally foggy or slow, like your brain's wrapped in cotton
- disconnected from people and things you usually care about
- emotionally flat—no highs, no lows, just nothing
- pulled toward your phone or sleep, not because it helps, but because it's easy

This isn't laziness. It's not about being unmotivated or careless. Shutdown is what happens when your system's been overstimulated, overloaded, or emotionally tapped out for too long. It's your brain trying to protect you by going dim. And while that makes sense short-term, staying stuck in that mode for too long can make it harder to climb back out.

Why It Happens

Shutdown doesn't come out of nowhere. Sometimes it's the result of emotional burnout—too many decisions, expectations, or disappointments without a break. Other times, it builds slowly from social exhaustion, feeling disconnected, or never feeling like you're doing "enough."

It can also be triggered by loneliness, performance pressure, constant comparison, or just carrying more than your mind knows how to process. And the longer it simmers, the harder it can be to explain.

That's part of why it's so tricky. You don't always notice it's happening until you feel completely stuck.

What Helps

Climbing out of shutdown isn't about pushing harder. It's about gently reconnecting to yourself, to the world around you, and to something that feels real again.

- **Start by noticing it:** Say it clearly: *"I think I've shut down."* Naming it gives you something solid to work with. It breaks the fog just enough to make a move.
- **Lower the bar seriously:** Don't try to fix everything. Ask yourself, *"What's one small thing I can do right now?"* Take a shower. Change your shirt. Text someone back. Small steps matter more than you think—especially when your system's on low battery.

- **Do something physical:** Shutdown often disconnects your mind from your body. So reintroduce movement, even in a low-stakes way. Stretch. Go outside. Walk around your block. Kick a ball against the wall. Movement doesn't need to be intense to help—it just needs to happen.
- **Change the scene:** Same room, same screen, same scroll? That keeps the loop going. Switch it up. Turn on a different playlist. Move to a new space. Clean off a corner of your desk. Even small changes in your environment can help your brain wake up and reset.
- **Connect with someone:** This one's big—even if it feels uncomfortable. Tell a friend, a sibling, a parent, a coach: *"I've been feeling off lately."* You don't need to give a TED Talk about your emotions. Just let someone know. It's easier to climb out of a fog when someone's willing to walk beside you.
- **Watch your self-talk:** Shutdown can bring in some harsh mental scripts: *"I'm lazy." "No one cares." "What's the point?"* None of those are facts—they're just signs you're overwhelmed. Try this instead: *"This isn't forever." "I'm just tired." "Small steps count."* Speak to yourself like someone worth taking care of—because you are.
- **Make one plan for the day:** It doesn't need to be a full to-do list. Just pick one thing. That plan becomes an anchor, something to help orient your brain when everything feels like floating.

Shutdown is a signal that your body and mind need something different—less noise, more care, more grounding. The goal isn't to go from zero to full blast overnight. It's to find your way back slowly, with gentleness and intention.

And if the fog lasts too long, or gets heavier instead of lighter? Reach out. You're not weak for needing support—you're smart for recognizing the signs and doing something about it.

YOU'RE NOT BROKEN

You're responding to life in real time, and sometimes the internal pressure builds faster than you can make sense of it. That doesn't mean you're dramatic, overreacting, or "too much." It means you're human—with a nervous system that's still figuring things out, a brain that's still wiring itself, and a world that doesn't always make it easy.

Emotions aren't a flaw to fix; they're feedback. The better you get at reading that feedback, the more power you have to respond in ways that match the kind of person you actually want to be.

And that kind of power? That's something most adults are still learning to use.

So the next time your head feels like static, your fuse runs short, or you just want to disappear for a while, pause. Tune in. Remind yourself: this doesn't define me; it just gives me information.

EIGHTEEN
FINDING A JOB AND MANAGING MONEY

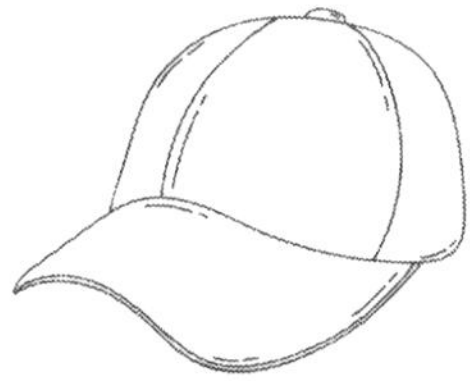

Learning how to handle money is one of the most useful skills you'll ever pick up. Sure, we usually talk about money like it's just about buying stuff, but it goes deeper than that. The way you earn and manage your money shapes your choices, opportunities, and freedom in ways that matter more than you might realize.

This doesn't mean you need a full financial plan by age 16. Nobody's expecting you to invest in stocks or budget like a CEO. What matters is that you start paying attention and build habits that make your life easier.

FIRST JOBS, REAL MONEY

Even a few hours a week at a job teach you how to manage your time, shows up when it matters, handles pressure, and deal with all kinds of people. That's real-life training.

Now, you don't need a degree, a suit, or a full résumé to get there. What *do* you need? A little effort and a bit of direction.

Start by thinking about what you're already good at and spot the kinds of jobs that are available for teens:

- **If you're good at school:**
  - Help younger students with their homework
  - Tutor classmates in subjects you've mastered
- **If you're handy or active:**
  - Mow lawns, rake leaves, shovel snow
  - Wash cars, walk dogs, pet-sit
  - Run errands for neighbors or older relatives
- **If you're creative or tech-savvy:**
  - Edit short videos or slideshows
  - Design birthday cards or posters
  - Flip sneakers, collectibles, or custom art
  - Help someone set up their phone or organize digital files
- **If you're organized:**
  - Assist with garage sales, home decluttering, or party setups
  - Volunteer to help at school events or sports games—sometimes it turns into paid work
- **Local gigs that teens actually get hired for:**
  - Weekends at cafés, food trucks, or market stalls
  - After-school hours at small shops or gyms
  - Seasonal or one-time help at community events

How to Get Hired With No Experience

1. **Start close to home:** Ask parents, neighbors, coaches, teachers, or friends of the family. A lot of

people will say yes to someone they trust, even if it's their first time doing the job.
2. **Say it simply:** You don't need a fancy pitch. Try: "Hi, I'm looking to earn a little and help out. Do you know anyone who might need an extra hand?"
3. **Make a one-page resume:** List your name, contact info, school, and a short section on what you've done—projects, responsibilities at home, anything that shows you're responsible. Keep it clear and clean.
4. **Follow up:** If someone says maybe, check back in a few days. That shows you're serious—and that alone can get you picked.

This isn't about finding your dream career. It's about getting started, building confidence, and learning how to earn on your own terms. That's a win, every time.

SAVING AND SPENDING

Now you've got some money. Doesn't matter if it came from chores, a weekend job, or your grandma's birthday card. Think of money like fuel: spend it all at once and you're stuck on the side of the road. Use it with purpose, and it'll get you where you want to go, without running out halfway there.

So, how do you make sure you're not running on empty?

Track It

Open your notes app, grab a cheap notebook, or find a simple app. Doesn't matter how, just start paying attention to what comes in and what goes out.

It doesn't need to look pretty. It just needs to be real. Because if you're not tracking your money, it's way too easy to lose sight of where it *actually* went (snacks, apps, random stuff you forgot five minutes later).

Even tracking for one week can open your eyes.

What Budgeting Really Means

Budgeting sounds like some adult spreadsheet thing. In reality, it's just a plan that helps you decide—before you spend—what your money should do.

Here's a simple breakdown that works for a lot of people starting out:

- **50% for essentials:** This covers stuff you *need* or are responsible for. Think transit, hygiene products, or helping with a family cost. If it keeps your life running, it goes here.
- **30% for spending:** This is your fun money—games, snacks, apps, going out, new gear, whatever lights you up.
- **20% for savings:** This is non-negotiable, even if it's $2.

A Word on Savings

Saving means making sure Future You isn't left scrambling because Now You spent it all on snacks or impulse buys. When you save, you're giving yourself options: the freedom to handle unexpected costs, jump on opportunities without panic, or make choices based on what you really want instead of what's cheapest right now.

Here's what saving can look like in real life:

- **Short-term:** Stuff you'll want sooner, like game credits, a weekend plan, or a new hoodie.
- **Medium-term:** Things that need a bit more time to save for, like a phone, a bike, or a laptop.
- **Long-term:** Big dreams and goals like a car, a trip, college costs, or your first apartment.

The goal is to be aware. Savings is part of your budget *because* it's part of your life. The more you build that muscle now, the more options you'll have later.

BANK BASICS

At first, getting paid in straight-up cash feels awesome. You can see it, count it, stuff it in your pocket. But the more you earn, the more you might start wondering: *Where do I even keep all this?*

What You Might Use Next

If you want your money to feel safer, more organized, and ready for bigger moves later on, it helps to know what else is out there.

PREPAID CARDS

These work kind of like gift cards—but for your own money. You load them up with cash, then use them to buy things online or in stores, without needing a full-on bank account. They're great if you're just getting started and want to keep things simple.

Teen Banking Apps

Some apps are made for teens and come with their own debit card. You can track spending, set savings goals, and see where your money's going—all from your phone. These usually link to a parent's account and come with limits (which actually helps you learn to manage it).

Real Bank Accounts

When your money starts stacking or you're saving for something big, you might want a regular bank account. There are two main types you'll probably hear about:

- **Checking account:** This one's for spending. It usually comes with a debit card you can swipe or use online. It's where your everyday money lives.
- **Savings account:** This one's built for the money you want to keep safe and untouched. It's not as easy to dip into, which is a kind of the point, and some of them even pay you interest just for keeping your money there.

If or when you decide to open a bank account, here's what you'll usually need:

- A *parent or guardian* to co-sign (banks require it for anyone under 18)
- A form of ID, like a school ID or passport
- Your *address*
- Your *Social Security Number* (in the U.S.)
- A small *starting amount* (some banks only ask for $25–$50)

Some banks have special teen accounts with no fees and easy mobile access, so you can check your balance, set savings goals, and track spending all from your phone.

Financial Habits That Make You a Boss

Good money habits are built overnight. So, before we wrap is important you understand that making and understanding money is step one. To really develop your money mindset, here's your starter pack for being financially sharp:

- **Be a saver:** Before you buy, save. If you can't afford it right now, press pause. That kind of patience is rare—and powerful. Over time, it builds the kind of confidence that doesn't shake every time you see a flashy ad or a limited-time sale.
- **Avoid impulse buys:** Sales are designed to rush you. Don't fall for it. Ask yourself: *Would I still want this next week?* If not, skip it. Smart spending isn't about being cheap—it's about making every dollar count.
- **Invest time in learning:** Money's a skill, not just a number. The more you know, the better your choices. Skip the fake-rich influencers flexing Lambos they rented. Look for real educators who explain money clearly. The better you understand how money moves, the less likely it is to move *away* from you.
- **Avoid debt:** Credit cards and loans might sound like free money, but they're not. Borrowing without knowing the rules can trap you in bills you can't pay back. Unless your parents are walking you through it or it's an emergency, steer clear for now. You've got time to learn it the right way.

Building these habits early isn't just impressive—it's game-changing. Most adults wish they'd started sooner. You actually can.

That's powerful.

QUIZ: LEVEL UP YOUR LIFE

Answer each question honestly—no need to flex. When you're done, head to the back of the book and see how you scored.

1. **Which statement best sums up a growth mindset?**
   a. Talent is fixed—if you're not good at something, avoid it
   b. You can improve through effort, learning, and time
   c. Success comes down to luck, not practice
2. **What's the difference between values and morals?**
   a. Values are personal priorities; morals are a shared sense of right and wrong
   b. Morals are personal; values are general
   c. They're basically the same thing
3. **In goal-setting, SMART stands for:**
   a. Specific, Measurable, Achievable, Relevant, Time-Bound
   b. Simple, Motivational, Active, Realistic, Tested
   c. Special, Measured, Awesome, Risky, Timed
4. **What's one good money habit to build early?**
   a. Spend first, think later
   b. Save a portion of what you earn before spending
   c. Keep all your cash handy for impulse buys
5. **What's the main benefit of having a budget?**
   a. It helps you plan how to use your money before you spend it
   b. You never have to say no to anything you want
   c. You can spend randomly without guilt

6. **Which set lists the Three C's of decision-making from the book?**
   a. Clarify, consider, choose
   b. Create, commit, celebrate
   c. Collect, compare, commit
7. **When you realize you've messed up, the first recommended step is to:**
   a. Deny it happened
   b. Call it what it is and own the mistake
   c. Blame someone else right away
8. **Working a first part-time job mainly teaches you to:**
   a. Manage your time, handle pressure, and deal with different people
   b. Earn huge money fast
   c. Avoid responsibility and chill

ANSWER KEYS

PART I ANSWERS

1. **B**) The hypothalamus signals the pituitary gland
2. **C**) Testosterone
3. **B**) Your body is growing unevenly and fast
4. **A**) Your body is adjusting to new physical abilities
5. **C**) Feeling more intense moods than usual
6. **B**) It expects guys to hide emotions and act tough all the time
7. **B**) It blames women for men's problems
8. **B**) Giving everyone equal rights and respect

PART II ANSWERS

1. **B**) Condoms
2. **A**) Many STIs show zero symptoms, so testing is the only way to know

3. **B)** A yes given while confused, pressured, or scared
4. **B)** Sex with someone below the legal age of consent—even if they say yes
5. **B)** Demanding your phone password and constant updates
6. **B)** An excited, pressure-free yes that can change at any time
7. **B)** Cuddling or talking to be sure both people feel comfortable
8. **A)** Outercourse (kissing, grinding, mutual masturbation)

PART III ANSWERS

1. **B)** To make money by selling your attention to advertisers
2. **B)** You compare yourself to filtered, "perfect" images and feel you don't measure up
3. **B)** Always ask the person's permission before you hit post, forward, or screenshot
4. **B)** A screenshot—or even a second phone—can preserve the image forever
5. **B)** Scenes are scripted performances that skip genuine consent, conversation, and after-care
6. **B)** Controlling behavior and a major red flag
7. **A)** Turning off non-essential notifications and creating no-phone zones
8. **B)** A serious violation of your privacy and digital consent

PART IV ANSWERS

1. **B**) Dopamine
2. **B**) It slows brain development and weakens decision-making
3. **B**) Marketing makes it look harmless, but the nicotine dose hits the brain fast
4. **B**) Five or more drinks in about two hours
5. **B**) Skipping sleep, school, or friends to keep playing
6. **B**) Say, "No thanks, I'm good," and change the subject
7. **B**) A minor-league mess-up that still brings real consequences
8. **B**) Reaching out to counselors, hotlines, or trusted adults

PART V ANSWERS

1. **B**) You can improve through effort, learning, and time
2. **A**) Values are personal priorities; morals are a shared sense of right and wrong
3. **A**) Specific, Measurable, Achievable, Relevant, Time-Bound
4. **B**) Save a portion of what you earn before spending
5. **A**) It helps you plan how to use your money before you spend it
6. **A**) Clarify, Consider, Choose
7. **B**) Call it what it is and own the mistake
8. **A**) Manage your time, handle pressure, and deal with different people

NINETEEN
KEEP GROWING, KEEP SHOWING UP

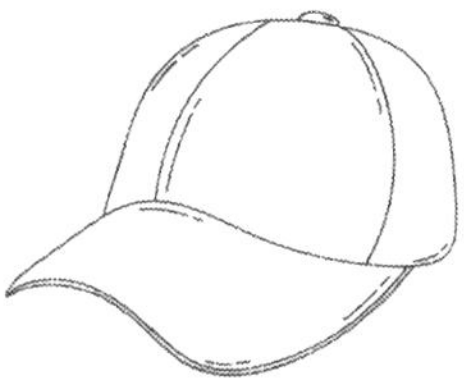

You made it—Congrats! That's huge! Most people would rather scroll past the awkward stuff than sit with it. But you didn't. You showed up, page after page, and faced some real talk about your body, your choices, and what kind of guy you want to be. That takes guts.

Growing up can feel like being dropped into a game with zero instructions and a glitchy tutorial. You're hit with hormones, expectations, TikToks telling you to "man up," and a bunch of people acting like you're just supposed to know how it all works. Spoiler: no one does at first. That's exactly why this book exists.

It wasn't here to give you every answer or turn you into a flawless, grown-up version of yourself overnight. The goal was simple: hand you tools that actually work. Stuff that helps you feel a little less confused and a lot more capable. Along the way, you've picked up some solid life XP. Like how to:

- understand what consent actually means
- deal with puberty without freaking out

- think critically about porn, social media, and screen time
- spot the early signs of addiction (and know what to do)
- handle peer pressure without becoming a clone
- build confidence that's quiet, not loud
- deal with anger, anxiety, and emotional shut-downs
- navigate dating, friendships, and your own identity
- recognize toxic masculinity when it tries to mess with your head
- talk about sex, masturbation, and protection without weirdness
- speak up when something's not okay
- ask for help without thinking, it makes you weak

Being a "stand-up dude" doesn't mean being perfect or always having it together. It means showing up with respect, asking questions when you're unsure, and taking responsibility when you mess up.

You'll still stumble—everyone does. What matters most is what happens next. Will you learn, take accountability, and move forward stronger? If you do, you're already miles ahead.

Keep being curious. Keep listening. And when life feels messy—whether it's about relationships, identity, emotions, or anything else—reach out to someone trustworthy. Talk to a parent, teacher, coach, counselor, or friend who genuinely listens. You don't have to figure it out alone—even when it feels like you do.

If you remember anything, let it be this: becoming your best self doesn't start "someday." It starts now—with how you treat people, with what you stand for and with the choices you make when no one's watching.

So keep your head up, your heart open, and keep showing up.

You've got this.

BIBLIOGRAPHY

A beginner's guide to goal setting for teens. (2020, May 13). Powerful Youth. https://powerfulyouth.com/beginners-guide-goal-setting-for-teens-smart-goals/

Adams, R. (2022, January 2). *What to spend money on & things to save up for as a teenager.* Youngandtheinvested.com. https://youngandtheinvested.com/things-to-save-up-for-as-teenager/

Advisible, Z. (2023, March 24). *Vocational education vs higher education.* 1300apprentice. https://1300apprentice.com.au/vocational-education-vs-higher-education/

Ali, M. (2022, May 24). *The science of visualization: Can imagining your goals make you more likely to accomplish them?* Neurovine. https://www.neurovine.ai/blog/the-science-of-visualization-can-imagining-your-goals-make-you-more-likely-to-accomplish-them#:~:text=Visualizing%20the%20scenario%20of%20succeeding

Aljanabi, K. (2024, August 12). Council post: Embrace nonlinear careers to redefine success in A dynamic world. *Forbes.* https://www.forbes.com/councils/forbescoachescouncil/2024/05/28/embrace-nonlinear-careers-to-redefine-success-in-a-dynamic-world/

Amy. (2023, October 18). Breaking into the world of freelancing: A beginner's guide. *Workfree.* https://workfree.io/blog/breaking-into-the-world-of-freelancing-a-beginners-guide

Andersson, K., Odlind, V., & Rybo, G. (1994). Levonorgestrel-releasing and copper-releasing (nova T) iuds during five years of use: A randomized comparative trial. *Contraception*, 49(1), 56–72. https://doi.org/10.1016/0010-7824(94)90109-0

Anxiety in teenagers. (2019, February). Raising Children Network. https://raisingchildren.net.au/pre-teens/mental-health-physical-health/stress-anxiety-depression/anxiety

Anzilotti, A. (2018). *HIV and AIDS.* Kidshealth.org. https://kidshealth.org/en/teens/std-hiv.html

Architecture and Engineering Occupations: Occupational Outlook Handbook: (2019, February 20). U.S. Bureau of Labor Statistics. https://www.bls.gov/ooh/architecture-and-engineering/home.htm

Arts and design occupations: Occupational outlook handbook. (2019, September 4). U.S. Bureau of Labor Statistics. https://www.bls.gov/ooh/arts-and-design/home.htm

Balk, M. (2022). Vision boards: What are they & how to create one in 5 steps. *Betterup.com.* https://www.betterup.com/blog/how-to-create-vision-board#:~:text=Finding%20images%20and%20words%20that

Batdorf, E. (2024, July 10). *Best teen checking accounts in July 2024.* CNN Underscored. https://edition.cnn.com/cnn-underscored/money/best-teen-checking-accounts

Birth control methods. (2019, February 14). Office on Women's Health. https://www.womenshealth.gov/a-z-topics/birth-control-methods

Birth control options & types: Risks & effectiveness. (2022, August 18). Cleveland Clinic. https://my.clevelandclinic.org/health/articles/11427-birth-control-options

Body dysmorphic disorder (BDD) and youth. (n.d.). Mental Health America. https://mhanational.org/body-dysmorphic-disorder-bdd-and-youth

Body Dysmorphic Disorder (for Parents) . (2018). Kidshealth.org. https://kidshealth.org/en/parents/bdd.html

Both teen girls and boys take and send nudes. (n.d.). Fight the New Drug. https://fightthenewdrug.org/uncovering-sexting-culture-in-rising-generation/

Brown, M. (2021, June 7). Your teen, yes yours, is sexting! Here's how to deal. *Psych Central.* https://psychcentral.com/blog/teens-sex-and-technology

Cabello, M. (2024, March 27). *The best places to save your money: Money market accounts, savings accounts and CDs.* Bankrate. https://www.bankrate.com/banking/savings/money-market-vs-savings-accounts-vs-cds/#differences

Castrillon, C. (2023, February 26). Why non-linear career paths are the future. *Forbes.* https://www.forbes.com/sites/carolinecastrillon/2023/02/26/why-non-linear-career-paths-are-the-future/

Cervical mucus: Chart, stages, tracking & fertility. (2021). Cleveland Clinic. https://my.clevelandclinic.org/health/body/21957-cervical-mucus

Cherry, K. (2023, September 28). *This is what's actually happening in your brain when you fall in love.* Verywell Mind. https://www.verywellmind.com/what-happens-in-your-brain-when-you-fall-in-love-7971808

Chlamydia. (2018). Kidshealth.org. https://kidshealth.org/en/teens/std-chlamydia.html

Chlamydia -CDC Fact Sheet. (n.d.). https://dpbh.nv.gov/uploadedFiles/dpbh.nv.gov/content/Programs/STD/dta/Publications/Chlamydia.pdf

Chloe. (2023, August 19). *The psychology of teenage love.* Psych2Go. https://psych2go.net/the-psychology-of-teenage-love/

Citron, D. K., & Franks, M. A. (2014, May 19). *Criminalizing revenge porn.* SSRN. https://papers.ssrn.com/sol3/papers.cfm?abstract_id=2368946

Collins, J. (2024, March). *What is teenage angst, and is it normal?* Clear Behavioral Health. https://clearbehavioralhealth.com/teenage-angst/

Common Sense Media. (2023, January 10). *New report reveals truths about how teens engage with pornography*. PR NewsWire. https://www.prnewswire.com/news-releases/new-report-reveals-truths-about-how-teens-engage-with-pornography-301717607.html?utm_source=chatgpt.com

Community and Social Service Occupations: Occupational Outlook Handbook. (2019, September 4). U.S. Bureau of Labor Statistics. https://www.bls.gov/ooh/community-and-social-service/home.htm

Computer and information technology occupations. (2023, September 6). U.S. Bureau of Labor Statistics. https://www.bls.gov/ooh/computer-and-information-technology/home.htm

Condom use: An overview. (2024, May 9). U.S. Centers for Disease Control and Prevention. https://www.cdc.gov/condom-use/?CDC_AAref_Val=https://www.cdc.gov/condomeffectiveness/docs/Condoms_and_STDS.pdf

Cramer, M. (2024, October 20). Number of young people accused of serious crimes surges in new york city. *The New York Times*. https://www.nytimes.com/2024/10/20/nyregion/youth-crime-arrests-nyc.html

Dalla-Camina, M. (2023, January 16). *6 steps to create your vision board (+ the neuroscience on why they work)*. Women Rising. https://womenrisingco.com/articles/6-steps-to-create-your-vision-board-the-neuroscience-on-why-they-work/#:~:text=Neuroscientist%20Dr.

Danao, M. (2023, April 20). 11 essential soft skills in 2023 (with examples). *Forbes Advisor*. https://www.forbes.com/advisor/business/soft-skills-examples/

Definition of CONTRACEPTION. (n.d.). Merriam-Webster. https://www.merriam-webster.com/dictionary/contraception

Discover your personal values. (n.d.). Personal Values. https://personalvalu.es/personal-values-test

Dixon, T. (2017, October 31). *Key studies: Dopamine and love (Fisher et al. 2005)*. IB Psychology. https://www.themantic-education.com/ibpsych/2017/11/01/key-studies-dopamine-and-love-fisher-2005/#google_vignette

Dunkley, C. R., & Brotto, L. A. (2019). The role of consent in the context of BDSM. *Sexual Abuse*, 32(6), 107906321984284. https://doi.org/10.1177/1079063219842847

Dunn, S., Guilbert, É., Burnett, M., Aggarwal, A., Bernardin, J., Clark, V., Davis, V., Dempster, J., Fisher, W., MacKinnon, K., Pellizzari, R., Polomeno, V., Rutherford, M., Sabourin, J., Senikas, V., & Wagner, M.-S. (2012). Emergency contraception. *Journal of Obstetrics and Gynaecology Canada*, 34(9), 870–878. https://doi.org/10.1016/s1701-2163(16)35387-7

Education, training, and library occupations: Occupational outlook handbook. (2019, April 12). U.S. Bureau of Labor Statistics. https://www.bls.gov/ooh/education-training-and-library/home.htm

Ericson, C. (2023, February 24). *Teen dating apps and online safety: What parents need to know.* Your Teen Magazine. https://yourteenmag.com/social-life/teen-dating-apps

Examples of passions and interests turned into success careers. (2024, January 9). Alton Road Digital. https://altonroaddigital.com/brand-pro-tips/5-examples-of-people-who-turned-passions-and-interests-into-successful-careers

Fardouly, J., Diedrichs, P. C., Vartanian, L. R., & Halliwell, E. (2015). Social comparisons on social media: The impact of facebook on young women's body image concerns and mood. *Body Image*, 13(1), 38–45. https://doi.org/10.1016/j.bodyim.2014.12.002

Farrell, M. (2023, January 6). *Data and intuition: Good decisions need both.* Harvard Business Publishing. https://www.harvardbusiness.org/data-and-intuition-good-decisions-need-both/

Feldman, R. (2012). Oxytocin and social affiliation in humans. *Hormones and Behavior*, 61(3), 380–391. https://doi.org/10.1016/j.yhbeh.2012.01.008

Felman, A. (2020, September 25). *Sexually transmitted infections (stis): Types and symptoms.* Medical News Today. https://www.medicalnewstoday.com/articles/sexually-transmitted-diseases

Fortenberry, J. D. (2013). Puberty and adolescent sexuality. *Hormones and Behavior*, 64(2), 280–287. https://doi.org/10.1016/j.yhbeh.2013.03.007

Fradd, M. (2015, April 10). 10 shocking stats about teens and pornography. *Covenant Eyes.* https://www.covenanteyes.com/blog/10-shocking-stats-about-teens-and-pornography/

Freedman, B., & Padian, N. (2000, November 30). *Barrier methods.* Division of Prevention Science. https://prevention.ucsf.edu/research-project/barrier-methods

From minor offenses to major crimes: What you need to know about felonies and misdemeanors. (2024, January 10). Barbieri Law. https://barbierilawfirm.com/2024/01/from-minor-offenses-to-major-crimes-what-you-need-to-know-about-felonies-and-misdemeanors/

Genital Warts (HPV). (n.d.). Kidshealth.org. https://kidshealth.org/en/teens/std-wart s.html

Gonorrhea. (2018). Kidshealth.org. https://kidshealth.org/en/teens/std-gonor rhea.html

Gupta, S. (n.d.). *Generation alpha is coming. their top career choices may surprise you.*

Fast Company. https://www.fastcompany.com/90806197/generation-alpha-top-career-choices-post-gen-z

Haelle, T. (2018, February 27). That teen sexting study: What else you need to know before freaking out. *Forbes*. https://www.forbes.com/sites/tarahaelle/2018/02/27/that-teen-sexting-study-what-else-you-need-to-know-before-freaking-out/

Hansen, R. S. (2024). *Non-traditional careers*. Metropolitan Community College. https://www.mccneb.edu/Student-Resources/TRIO/Non-Traditional-Careers

Healthcare occupations: Occupational outlook handbook. (2018, April 13). U.S. Bureau of Labor Statistics. https://www.bls.gov/ooh/healthcare/home.htm

Hepatitis B. (n.d.). Kidshealth.org. https://kidshealth.org/en/teens/std-hepatitis.html

Hinduja, S., & Patchin, J. (2018). *Teen sexting: A brief guide for educators and parents*. Cyberbullying Research Centre. https://www.hill.af.mil/Portals/58/documents/DAVA/Sexting-Research-Summary-4-Parents.pdf

Hirsch, L. (2016). *Female reproductive system (for parents)*. KidsHealth. https://kidshealth.org/en/parents/female-reproductive-system.html

Hirsch, L. (2018). *The diaphragm (for teens)*. KidsHealth. https://kidshealth.org/en/teens/contraception-diaphragm.html

Hirsch, L. (2019). *Male reproductive system (for parents)*. KidsHealth. https://kidshealth.org/en/parents/male-reproductive.html

Holland, G., & Tiggeman, M. (2016). A systematic review of the impact of the use of social networking sites on body image and disordered eating outcomes. *Body Image*, 17(1), 100–110. https://doi.org/10.1016/j.bodyim.2016.02.008

How do predators find children online? (n.d.). *Beau Biden Foundation*. https://www.beaubidenfoundation.org/onlinepredatorsblog1/

How effective are IUDs? (2019). Planned Parenthood. https://www.plannedparenthood.org/learn/birth-control/iud/how-effective-are-iuds

How to apply to colleges: Tips to get started. (n.d.). BigFuture. https://bigfuture.collegeboard.org/plan-for-college/apply-to-college/college-applications-how-to-begin

How to know if I am ready for sex. (n.d.). Planned Parenthood. https://www.plannedparenthood.org/learn/teens/sex/all-about-sex/am-i-ready-sex

How to talk about birth control with your teenager. (2024, April 3). West Des Moines OBGYN. https://www.westdesmoinesobgyn.com/how-to-talk-about-birth-control-with-your-teenager/

How to use a male condom (for teens). (2024, January). Kidshealth.org. https://kidshealth.org/en/teens/condom-directions.html

Howard, S. A., & Benhabbour, S. R. (2023). Non-Hormonal contraception. *Journal of Clinical Medicine*, 12(14), 4791. https://doi.org/10.3390/jcm12144791

Javed, A. (2024, September 16). *15+ social media recruitment statistics you have to know*. Qureos. https://www.qureos.com/hiring-guide/social-media-recruitment-statistics#:~:text=ASAP

Jia-Hui, C., & Xiao-Ying, Y. (2021). Effects of copper-containing intrauterine devices on the endometrium. *Reproductive and Developmental Medicine*, 05(01), 38–43. https://doi.org/10.4103/2096-2924.309791

Joshi, D. (2021, September). *10 tips for helping teens navigate the world of online dating and relationships*. The Fox Magazine. https://thefoxmagazine.com/technology/10-tips-for-helping-teens-navigate-the-world-of-online-dating-and-relationships/

Kabotyanski, K. E., & Somerville, L. H. (2021). Puberty: Your brain on hormones. *Frontiers for Young Minds*, 8. https://doi.org/10.3389/frym.2020.554380

Kaplan, Z. (2023, October 19). How to choose a career: 6 steps, plus a free quiz. *Forage*. https://www.theforage.com/blog/basics/how-to-choose-career

Kaunitz, A. M. (1989). Injectable contraception. *Clinical Obstetrics and Gynecology*, 32(2), 356–368. https://doi.org/10.1097/00003081-198906000-00020

Khanna, B. (2023, September 28). *The skills you need to stay ahead of the curve in 2030*. Linkedin.com. https://www.linkedin.com/pulse/skills-you-need-stay-ahead-curve-2030-bhupendra-khanna/

Kraus, S. W., Voon, V., & Potenza, M. N. (2016). Should compulsive sexual behavior be considered an addiction? *Addiction*, *111*(12), 2097–2106. https://doi.org/10.1111/add.13297

Kraut, M. (2023). *Juvenile offenses*. Child Crime Prevention & Safety Center. https://childsafety.losangelescriminallawyer.pro/juvenile-offenses.html

Larkin, T., & Thomas, S. J. (n.d.). 2023: *What happens in our brain and body when we're in love?* University of Wollongong. https://www.uow.edu.au/media/2023/what-happens-in-our-brain-and-body-when-were-inlove.php

Legal occupations: Occupational outlook handbook. (2019, September 4). U.S. Bureau of Labor Statistics. https://www.bls.gov/ooh/legal/home.htm

Lockwood, P., & Cutler, J. (2022, September 30). Why do teenagers take more risks? *Psychology Today*. https://www.psychologytoday.com/us/blog/the-helpful-brain/202209/why-do-teenagers-take-more-risks

Mancini, J. (2023, March 31). How to start a business as a teenager. *Doola: Start Your Dream US Business and Keep It 100% Compliant*. https://www.doola.com/blog/how-to-start-a-business-as-a-teenager/

Marcin, A. (2015, December). *The stages of puberty: Development in girls and boys*. Healthline. https://www.healthline.com/health/parenting/stages-of-puberty

Mayo Clinic Staff. (2022, February 16). *Birth control options: Things to consider*. Mayo Clinic. https://www.mayoclinic.org/healthy-lifestyle/birth-control/in-depth/birth-control-options/art-20045571 mediaer. (2024, June 25). *Young people, body image and social media.* The Digital Wellness Lab. https://digitalwellnesslab.org/research-briefs/social-media-body-image/

Miller, C. (n.d.). *Depression and anger.* Child Mind Institute. https://childmind.org/article/depression-and-anger/

Motivating a teenager: 15 steps that work! (2022). Liahona Academy. https://www.liahonaacademy.com/motivating-teenager-15-steps-that-work.html

National Sexual Violence Resource center. (2010). *What is sexual violence?* https://www.nsvrc.org/sites/default/files/Publications_NSVRC_Factsheet_What-is-sexual-violence_1.pdf

Nindra, R. (2020, March 5). *Why it's better to be open to a change in your career goal.* Linkedin. https://www.linkedin.com/pulse/why-its-better-open-change-your-career-goal-ryan-nindra/

Norman, W. V., Chiles, J. L., Turner, C. A., Brant, R., Aslan, A., & Kaczorowski, J. (2012). Comparing the effectiveness of copper intrauterine devices available in Canada. Is FlexiT non-inferior to NovaT when inserted immediately after first-trimester abortion? Study protocol for a randomized controlled trial. *Trials, 13*(1). https://doi.org/10.1186/1745-6215-13-147

Nuñez, C., & Pfeffer, L. (2016, July 21). *13 Amazing Coming of Age Traditions From Around the World.* Global Citizen. https://www.globalcitizen.org/en/content/13-amazing-coming-of-age-traditions-from-around-th/

Office for National Statistics. (2024, October 24). *Crime in England and Wales: year ending June 2024.* https://www.ons.gov.uk/peoplepopulationandcommunity/crimeandjustice/bulletins/crimeinenglandandwales/yearendingjune2024/pdf

Ott, M. A., & Sucato, G. S. (2014). Contraception for adolescents. *PEDIATRICS, 134*(4), e1257–e1281. https://doi.org/10.1542/peds.2014-2300

Ou, S.-R., & Reynolds, A. J. (2010). Childhood predictors of young adult male crime. *Children and Youth Services Review,* 32(8), 1097–1107. https://doi.org/10.1016/j.childyouth.2010.02.009

Our sweet story. (2019). Me & the Bees Lemonade. https://www.meandthebees.com/pages/about-us

Ovulation: Calculating, timeline, pain & other symptoms. (2022, August 7). Cleveland Clinic. https://my.clevelandclinic.org/health/articles/23439-ovulation

Oyibo, Y. (2023, July 24). How to understand different types of personalities like a pro. *Diary of an Introvert.* https://www.diaryofanintrovertng.com/blog/types-of-personalities

Pelvic inflammatory disease (PID). (n.d.). Kidshealth.org. https://kidshealth.org/en/teens/std-pid.html

Personality types. (2011). 16personalities.com; NERIS Analytics Limited. https://www.16personalities.com/personality-types

Pietrangelo, A. (2016, June 14). *12 things to know sex, emotions, and intimacy*. Healthline. https://www.healthline.com/health/healthy-sex/sex-emotions

Puberty: Tanner stages for boys and girls. (2023, September 5). Cleveland Clinic. https://my.clevelandclinic.org/health/body/puberty

Pubic lice (crabs). (n.d.). Kidshealth.org. https://kidshealth.org/en/teens/std-lice.html

Raina, P. (2024, July 18). *How to leverage linkedin with gen Z mindset*. Linkedin. https://www.linkedin.com/pulse/how-leverage-linkedin-gen-z-mindset-pooja-raina-tcikc/

RAINN. (2024). *Children and Teens: Statistics*. Rainn.org. https://rainn.org/statistics/children-and-teens

Raymond, V. (2018, February 14). *This is your body on love*. Right as Rain by UW Medicine. https://rightasrain.uwmedicine.org/life/relationships/your-body-love

Routledge international handbook of women's sexual and reproductive health. (2020). https://api.taylorfrancis.com/content/books/mono/download?identifierName=doi&identifierValue=10.4324/9781351035620&type=googlepdf

Samir. (2018). *Teen review: Teen tips for success in high school*. Typepad.com. https://torontopubliclibrary.typepad.com/teens/2018/09/teen-review-teen-tips-for-success-in-high-school.html

Sexual violence. (2024, July 19). Australian Institute of Health and Welfare; Australian Government. https://www.aihw.gov.au/family-domestic-and-sexual-violence/types-of-violence/sexual-violence

Sexually transmitted infections (STIs). (2023, July 10). World Health Organization. https://www.who.int/news-room/fact-sheets/detail/sexually-transmitted-infections-(stis)

Sherman, L. E., Payton, A. A., Hernandez, L. M., Greenfield, P. M., & Dapretto, M. (2016). The power of the like in adolescence: Effects of peer influence on neural and behavioral responses to social media. *Psychological Science*, 27(7), 1027–1035. https://doi.org/10.1177/0956797616645673

Shulyndina, E. (2021, February 11). Your guide to safe and private online dating. *Kaspersky.com; Kaspersky*. https://www.kaspersky.com/blog/dating-apps-privacy-and-safety/38754/

Staff Writers. (2020, March 11). 9 tips to increase college admission chances. *BestColleges*. https://www.bestcolleges.com/blog/tips-to-increase-college-admission-chances/

Stockton, T. (2021). *Can Visualization Improve Performance?* The Jackson Clinics. https://thejacksonclinics.com/can-visualization-improve-athletic-performance/#:~:text=In%20fact%2C%20the%20brain%20circuits

Support your teens in making career choices. (2022, December 16). Alberta Alis. https://alis.alberta.ca/tools-and-resources/resources-for-parents/resources-for-parents-help-your-children-plan-their-careers/support-your-teens-in-making-career-choices/

Supporting your teen as they navigate their future education and career journey. (2024). Question the Quo. https://www.questionthequo.org/insights/insights/supporting-your-teen-as-they-navigate-their-future-education-and-career-journey/

Sy, L. (2021, December 2). How to reach and engage gen Z on linkedin. *Linkedin.* https://www.linkedin.com/business/marketing/blog/trends-tips/how-does-gen-z-use-linkedin-and-what-types-of-content-resonate

Syphilis. (n.d.). Kidshealth.org. https://kidshealth.org/en/teens/std-syphilis.html

Talbot, C., & Boynton, E. (2023, February 13). *Brain chemistry influences love + attraction.* Right as Rain by UW Medicine. https://rightasrain.uwmedicine.org/life/relationships/brain-chemistry-influences-love

Teaching older children and teens about consent. (2024). Alberta. https://myhealth.alberta.ca/Health/pages/conditions.aspx?hwid=acm2222&lang=en-ca

Team Missy. (2024, January 16). *The emotional side of sex: Building healthy relationships.* Missy. https://missy.ie/the-emotional-side-of-sex-building-healthy-relationships/

The Bark Team. (2023, February 14). 2024 gen Z slang guide for dating and relationships. *Bark.* https://www.bark.us/blog/genz-slang-dating/

The face of global sex 2007 first sex: An opportunity of a lifetime netw rk. (2007). *Durex Network.* https://www.durexnetwork.org/SiteCollectionDocuments/Research%20-%20Face%20of%20Global%20Sex%202007.pdf

The growth spurt. (n.d.). BBC Home. https://www.bbc.co.uk/science/humanbody/body/articles/lifecycle/teenagers/growth.shtml

The science behind adolescent risk taking and exploration. (2023). Center for the Developing Adolescent. https://developingadolescent.semel.ucla.edu/topics/item/science-of-risk-taking

The wheel of motives: Towards a periodic table of human motivation . (2018). *Semantic Scholar.* https://www.semanticscholar.org/paper/The-THE-WHEEL-OF-MOTIVES-%3A-TOWARDS-A-PERIODIC-TABLE-Psicolog%C3%ADa/f758f42996c0a644ef715632a8206da1debfa040

Transportation and material moving occupations: Occupational outlook handbook. (2019, September 4). U.S. Bureau of Labor Statistics. https://www.bls.gov/ooh/transportation-and-material-moving/home.htm

Trichomoniasis. (n.d.). Kidshealth.org. https://kidshealth.org/en/teens/std-trichomoniasis.html

Trussell, J. (n.d.). Contraceptive efficacy. *Glob. Libr. Women's Med.*, 1756-2228. https://doi.org/10.3843/GLOWM.10375

Using the Holland codes for career planning. (2023, *August* 3). *Truity*. https://www.truity.com/blog/page/using-holland-codes-career-planning

videobypro. (2022, September 15). *Common sentiments that many teenage girls feel...* Kristi Newhouse. https://kristinewhouse.com/common-sentiments-that-many-teenage-girls-feel/

Vogels, E. (2022, December 15). *Teens and cyberbullying* 2022. Pew Research Center. https://www.pewresearch.org/internet/2022/12/15/teens-and-cyberbullying-2022/

Vogels, E. A., Gelles-Watnick, R., & Massarat, N. (2022, August 10). *Teens, social media and technology* 2022. Pew Research Center; Pew Research Center. https://www.pewresearch.org/internet/2022/08/10/teens-social-media-and-technology-2022/

Voon, V., Mole, T. B., Banca, P., Porter, L., Morris, L., Mitchell, S., Lapa, T. R., Karr, J., Harrison, N. A., Potenza, M. N., & Irvine, M. (2014). Neural correlates of sexual cue reactivity in individuals with and without compulsive sexual behaviours. *PLoS ONE*, 9(7), e102419. https://doi.org/10.1371/journal.pone.0102419

Wedekind, C., Seebeck, T., Bettens, F., & Paepke, A. J. (1995). MHC-dependent mate preferences in humans. *Proceedings. Biological Sciences*, 260(1359), 245–249. https://doi.org/10.1098/rspb.1995.0087

Weschler, T. (2015). Taking charge of your fertility. In *Google Books*. HarperCollins. My Book

What is sexting and is it common among teens? (2021). Brown University Health. https://www.brownhealth.org/be-well/what-sexting-and-it-common-among-teens

Wilson, A. (2023, June 14). *6 key reasons to stay relevant: Importance of remaining current in today's dynamic world*. Medium. https://medium.com/@TheAndrewLab/6-key-reasons-to-stay-relevant-importance-of-remaining-current-in-todays-dynamic-world-d8e0adae46e1

World Economic Forum. (2023). Future of jobs report 2023. In *World Economic Forum*. https://www3.weforum.org/docs/WEF_Future_of_Jobs_2023.pdf

World Population Clock. (2024). Worldometers. https://www.worldometers.info/world-population/

Worthy, L. D., Lavigne, T., & Romero, F. (2020, July 27). *Sexuality and culture*. Maricopa. https://open.maricopa.edu/culturepsychology/chapter/sexuality-and-culture/

You and your pregnancy at 1 to 3 weeks. (2020, December 1). NHS. https://www.nhs.uk/pregnancy/week-by-week/1-to-12/1-2-3-weeks/

Your guide to coping with an angry teenager. (2025, March 7). University of Utah Health. https://healthcare.utah.edu/healthfeed/2025/03/your-guide-coping-angry-teenager

Yuan, K. (2018, December 12). *How teens turned instagram into a dating app*. The Atlantic. https://www.theatlantic.com/membership/archive/2018/12/how-teens-turned-instagram-into-a-dating-app/578020/

ABOUT THE AUTHOR

REAL TALK LIBRARY

Real Talk Library is a co creation between a published author and professional documentary maker and journalist. It's a storytelling venture that spans fact and fiction, publishing high-quality books including a recently published thriller called The Tunnel and teen-focused titles The New Sex Education for Teens and The Complete Guide to Modern Manhood.

Candida Beveridge (The New Sex Education for Teens and The Complete Guide to Modern Manhood) is an award-winning journalist and documentary filmmaker. She has produced and directed across the globe — from the jungles of Borneo and mountains of Bhutan to immersive shoots in Bangladesh and the Philippines. Her credits span documentary, factual and reality genres, appearing on platforms such as Netflix, National Geographic, Discovery, Apple TV+, Canal +, BBC TV & Radio, Channel 4, ITV, TVNZ, Prime (New Zealand), Neon (NZ), The Guardian and The Daily Mail.

Toby Hill (The Tunnel) is a novelist specializing in true crime and revenge fantasies. He writes everything from screenplays and essays to the things you think but will never do. He holds a BA in philosophy, an MA in Creative Writing and masquerades as a builder. He splits his time between homes in Auckland and London travelling extensively in between.

If you liked this book, please leave a review on Amazon and help it get to more readers.

Printed in Dunstable, United Kingdom

76241774R00116